Higher

A B & W, the first airplane model produced by William Boeing and his partner, Navy Lt. George Conrad Westervelt, taxis across Seattle's Lake Union.

Passengers pose in front
of the Model 80, built by
Boeing Air Transport.
It was the first American
airliner designed with
passenger comfort in mind.

The advanced B-29
Superfortress (right) was
much larger than its
predecessor, the B-17
Flying Fortress (left).

The X-15 research rocket plane, built by North American Aviation, launches from its NASA B-52A mothership.

The Apollo 8 Saturn V spacecraft lifts off. It was the first manned spacecraft to orbit the moon, giving people on Earth a view of their planet from space.

F/A-18 Hornet Blue Angels fly in delta formation. In 1986, the U.S. Navy designated the F/A-18 the official Blue Angels jet.

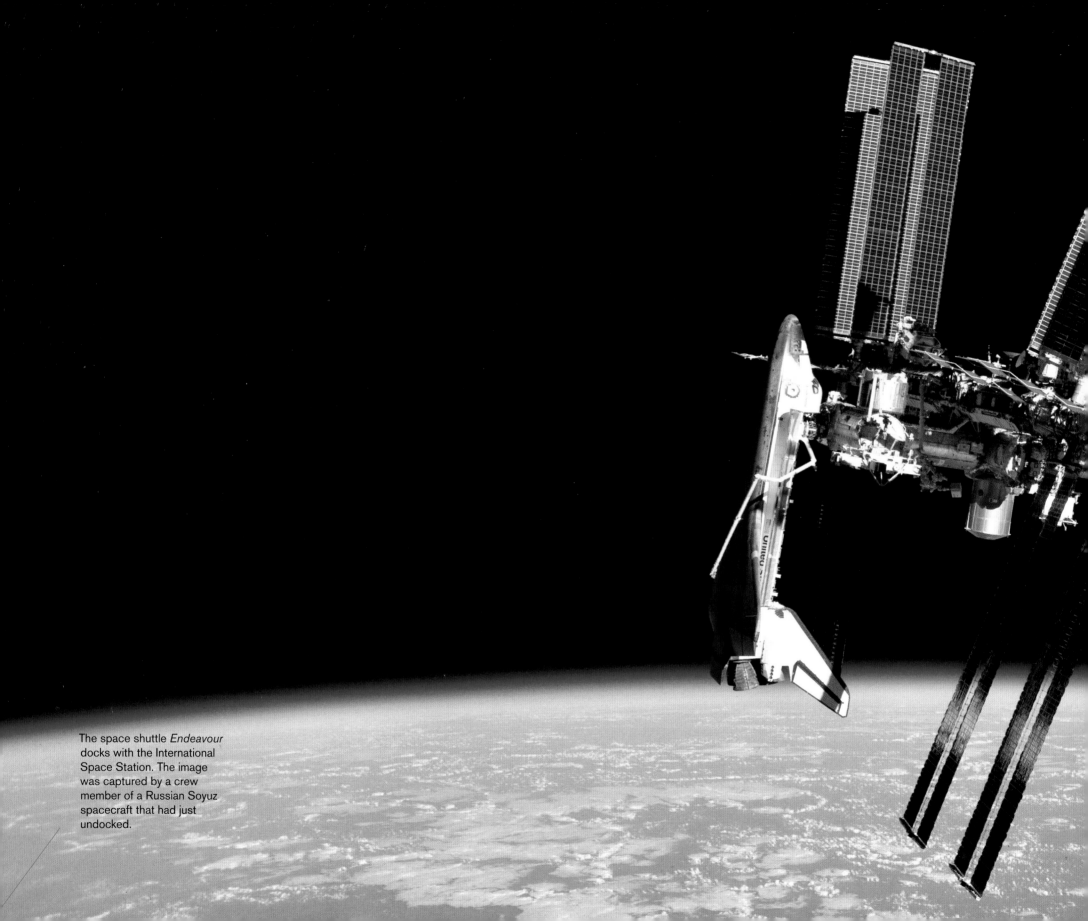

The space shuttle *Endeavour* docks with the International Space Station. The image was captured by a crew member of a Russian Soyuz spacecraft that had just undocked.

100 Years of Boeing

Higher

Russ Banham

CHRONICLE BOOKS
SAN FRANCISCO

Page 192 constitutes a continuation of the copyright page.

ISBN: 978-1-4521-4053-7

Library of Congress Cataloging-in-Publication data available.

Manufactured in China.
Designed by Zach Hooker.

FSC
www.fsc.org
MIX
Paper from
responsible sources
FSC® C104723

Permission to reproduce works of art, photographs, and artifacts
in this volume was provided by the rights holders, when they
could be identified. Every effort was made to obtain and verify
accurate identifying information for the works. Please notify The
Boeing Company of any inaccuracies, and corrections will be
included in future editions.

www.boeing.com

10 9 8 7 6 5 4 3 2

Chronicle Books LLC
680 Second Street
San Francisco, California 94107

www.chroniclebooks.com

Previous page: A 787-8
Dreamliner flies over the
Oregon coast.

Left: The CST-100 crew
capsule, shown in an
artist's rendering, is
Boeing's newest foray
into spaceflight.

CONTENTS

Introduction

In 1916, lumberman Bill Boeing built an airplane in a boathouse in Seattle and entered the brand-new field of aviation. One hundred years later, air travel is commonplace, and the name Boeing is synonymous with flight around the world

The story of how a small local company venturing into a new industry became a global household name is one of tremendous achievement and perseverance. The history of The Boeing Company is inseparable from that of human flight—from the early days of commercial aviation and strategic air power to the current age of jet travel and space exploration.

It is a story not just of great successes but also of struggles and setbacks. Within the aviation industry, Boeing engaged in bruising competition—and, when necessary, close collaboration—that spurred even greater triumphs. Today, Boeing and its former competitors—including Douglas Aircraft, McDonnell Aircraft, and parts of North American Aviation and Hughes Aircraft—are united as one global enterprise that is leading the field of aerospace into the future.

Above all, the Boeing story is about the many thousands of men and women who have demonstrated imagination, resilience, and tenacity in their quest to take humankind faster, farther, and higher than ever before.

A 737-700 banks in a sunlit sky. The 737 is the best-selling airliner in aviation history.

The Beginnings

At the turn of the 20th century, the world seemed like a much smaller place. Roads were unpaved and rutted, and most people got from here to there in a horse and buggy—"from here to there" being a distance of no more than 50 miles. For longer distances, travelers had the costly options of journeying by rail or ship. A trip across the United States took at least a week. A transatlantic journey from New York to Southampton, England, required a minimum of five days, and therefore such trips were not common.

Then, two brothers who operated a bicycle shop in Dayton, Ohio, demonstrated the feasibility of machine-powered human flight. The physical boundaries that held humans on the ground were conquered at last. Although the link between flight and travel was not immediate, the brothers' achievement would make long-distance travel accessible to the public in only a few years.

So extraordinary was the first sustained heavier-than-air human flight by Orville and Wilbur Wright on December 17, 1903, that French inventor and engineer Louis Bleriot wrote, "The most beautiful dream that has haunted the heart of man since Icarus is today reality." No one alive at the time would have disagreed.

Certainly not Bill Boeing. For this 23-year-old who had just left Sheffield Scientific School at Yale University, science and adventure were inextricably linked. Boeing had studied engineering at Yale and had a bent for "all things mechanical," an early biographer noted. He enjoyed testing his physical skills and stamina, racing boats and cars. His adventurous interests led him to Grays Harbor,

Washington, where he quickly learned the logging business on some timberland owned by his family.

Year by year, Boeing added to these holdings and traded them, gradually establishing himself in the Pacific Northwest as a sharp businessman, a "man on the go," in the parlance of the day. In 1908 he moved his operations to Seattle, where he founded the Greenwood Timber Company, joining a class of other timber barons including Frederick Weyerhaeuser and Jack Eddy. Still, something was missing, an undefined need to engage in a business that was more exciting than buying timberlands and cutting down spruce.

Perhaps this explains Boeing's business diversifications. His first was the acquisition in 1910 of the Heath Shipyard on the Duwamish River, where he had previously had a yacht called the *Taconite* built. Piloting the yacht appealed to his sense of adventure. So did the prospect of flying in an airplane, a longing he had harbored since the Wright brothers accomplished their historic feat a few years before.

In 1910, he traveled with friends to Los Angeles for the first International Air Meet. Transfixed by the aerial stunts and apparently unfazed by the danger, he approached French pilot Louis Paulhan and asked for a trip in his plane. Boeing didn't get a ride, but he was determined to get one the next time.

The opportunity came at a 1914 Fourth of July flying exhibition in Seattle. Lining up for a flight on aviator Terah Maroney's plane were Boeing and Navy Lieutenant George Conrad Westervelt, a close friend who had studied aeronautical engineering at the Massachusetts Institute of Technology (MIT) and shared his interest in aviation. Boeing went first, perching beside Maroney on the front edge of the biplane's lower muslin-covered wing. He later remarked that he could see the lake "tilting up beside him like a flat picture plate" as the plane banked away from Seattle's Lake Union.

Previous spread: The first B & W airplanes were built in a boathouse on Lake Union in Seattle.

Right: Timberman Bill Boeing rides a steamer ship into Grays Harbor, Washington, in 1903, the same year the Wright brothers achieved flight.

The aircraft ascended farther into the sky, and Boeing witnessed the grand scenery of Puget Sound and "tiny people" below, his friend Westervelt among them. The ride was soon over, and the plane's pontoons skidded across the lake's surface. Afterward, Boeing turned to Westervelt and said, "There isn't much to that machine of Maroney's. I think we could build a better one." Westervelt agreed.

Boeing decided to learn how to pilot a plane himself and signed up for flying lessons at the Glenn L. Martin Flying School in Los Angeles. Upon receiving his license, he purchased a Martin TA floatplane in which to practice flying. It arrived in pieces in crates, and he had it assembled in his boathouse on the shores of Lake Union. But he was no more impressed with the Martin TA than with Maroney's biplane.

Armed with Westervelt's knowledge of aerodynamics and Boeing's mechanical skills, the two men tackled the task of making a better plane. They replaced the single pontoon on the Martin TA with two pontoons affixed to two outriggers—an innovation that enhanced stability during takeoff and landing. Westervelt arranged for his alma mater to review the design and test a model of the twin-float seaplane in MIT's brand-new four-foot-wide wind tunnel on Vassar Street in Cambridge. It passed with flying colors.

From these humble beginnings—two fellows in a small boathouse making a better airplane— sprang the company that would make passenger air travel routine and voyages to the moon attainable.

The partners called their plane the B & W for their respective initials. The first model was chris-

tened the *Bluebill.* Soon, the second (and final) B & W, the *Mallard,* was in production. Boeing recruited about a dozen workers for the new aircraft company, including pilots, carpenters, boat builders, and seamstresses to sew together the muslin wing coverings. They manufactured the aircraft one piece at a time at the shipyard on the Duwamish River and trucked the pieces to Boeing's boathouse for assembly.

On June 29, 1916, the *Bluebill* made its maiden flight, without Westervelt there to watch it. The country was on the brink of war, and the U.S. Navy had dispatched him to the East Coast to prepare for maneuvers. At the controls of the plane was Bill Boeing—the pilot was late, and Boeing had a yearning to fly it anyway. He taxied the plane along the waters of Lake Union, gunned the engine, and lifted off for a brief quarter-mile trip. Years later, *Boeing* magazine would describe the *Bluebill* on its first flight: "its wings straight and pert, spruce struts gleaming with new varnish."

Upon landing, Boeing remarked, "The construction was better all around [than the Martin TA]." As he had predicted, they had made a better plane.

With Westervelt gone, Boeing incorporated Pacific Aero Products Co. on his own on July 15, 1916. The following year, he changed the name of the aircraft manufacturing company to Boeing Airplane Co. He was convinced that constant innovation and technological advancements were the keys to making the company a success, and he was willing to spend what it took to achieve it.

To attain his objectives, Boeing hired one of the few aeronautical engineers in the country, Wong

A B & W is shown in flight in a painting by Boeing artist Fred Takasumi (left).

This photograph of a B & W in the air gives a clear view of the seaplane's pontoons.

Tsoo, a Chinese national studying in the United States. Other engineers, including Clairmont "Claire" Egtvedt and Philip G. Johnson, both recent graduates from the University of Washington, also joined the company. By the end of its first year of existence, Boeing Airplane Co. had almost 30 employees.

From the beginning, Boeing had a reputation as an exacting perfectionist. He was well aware of the seriousness of his new enterprise—people's lives were at stake. He once saw a set of improperly sawed spruce ribs in the shipyard that served as the company's manufacturing plant and tossed them to the floor and broke them. Another time, he spied a frayed aileron cable and said, "I, for one, will close up shop rather than send out work of this kind." Bill Boeing's regard for meticulousness is woven into the history of the company that bears his name and characterizes the enterprise to this day.

Despite the company's early commitment to quality and innovation, orders were slow in coming. To keep the business going, Boeing dug into his own wallet to guarantee a loan covering his payroll—about $700 a week, a huge sum at the time.

There was a break in the financial strains on the company when Westervelt wrote Boeing that the Navy desperately needed training planes to create a corps of pilots. The war in Europe had escalated, and the United States was preparing for probable involvement. Boeing immediately charged Wong to assist the company's lead engineer, James Foley, with designing a new aircraft to address the Navy's need. The result, the Model C seaplane, incorporated several mold-breaking innovations. The wings tilted upward two degrees, and the upper wing sat forward of the lower wing rather than being stacked. Wong tested a model of the plane in a wind tunnel that had just been built at the University of Washington; Boeing had funded its construction

in the hope that the school would eventually provide well-trained aeronautical engineers for the growing company. The aircraft performed beyond expectations.

Now, he had to get the plane to the Navy base in Pensacola, Florida, for evaluation before the deadline. Flying the plane from Seattle would take too long, so Boeing had two Model C planes dismantled and shipped by rail to Pensacola, accompanied by the Boeing factory superintendent, Claude Berlin, and a test pilot, Herb Munter. In Florida, Berlin reassembled one plane and Munter flew it for Navy officials, who were impressed and ordered 50 Model Cs. It was Boeing's first production order and a sizable one at that—a total of 56 Model C trainers ultimately were built.

The Navy also ordered 50 single-engine HS-2L patrol seaplanes, which were designed by Curtiss Aeroplane and Motor Co. and manufactured by Boeing and three other aircraft makers—a partnership among competing manufacturers that foreshadowed future collaborations during times of war and in the race to space.

To manufacture the two orders for Navy seaplanes, the workforce at Boeing had ballooned to 337 employees by 1918. But when the war ended that November, the Navy cut its order for HS-2Ls in half. New passenger airplanes weren't needed either—the surplus biplanes left over from the war were more than adequate. For the first time, Bill Boeing felt the business repercussions of the boom-and-bust cycle that would typify the industry.

A Boeing Model C awaits flight in Boeing's Lake Union boathouse in Seattle. The Navy would order 50 of the training planes as the United States entered World War I.

"The war ended, and so did business," Boeing's son, Bill Boeing Jr., later said. "Thankfully, my father still had a successful logging operation [to keep] all those good people in the shop."

Taking advantage of his timber holdings, Boeing had his idled workers build commercial and residential furniture and flat-bottomed speedboats called Sea Sleds—the "automobiles of the sea," according to the *Seattle Daily Times*. Although these were not the kinds of ventures he had in mind for the Boeing Airplane Co., he remained patient that the market would revive. As time wore on, the company struggled to survive.

In 1919, Boeing signed a modest contract with the U.S. Army to modernize 298 British-built de Havilland DH-4 fighter planes. Unable to get a line of credit from the banks, Boeing had to again dig into his wallet to pay for their manufacture. Layoffs soon became unavoidable, and the workforce dwindled to a fifth of its wartime size. Without another order for aircraft soon, Boeing confided to his vice president and general manager, Edgar N. Gott, he'd have to close up shop.

But as the new decade dawned, the company's prospects brightened. Commercial orders picked up, and Boeing was back making its own aircraft. The first order was for a new plane, the BB-L6, wanted by a local pilot to transport passengers on aerial tours—two at a time, sitting in front of him in the cockpit. The BB-L6 marked a new direction for the company: it was Boeing's first aircraft specifically designed to carry passengers.

The company also received an order for 200 open-cockpit biplanes from the fledgling U.S. Army Air Service (forerunner of the U.S. Air Force). The MB-3A fighter plane was designed by Thomas-Morse Aircraft Corporation, which manufactured the first 50 MB-3s. But when the Air Service put out a request for additional planes, Boeing's ready access to spruce to build the planes enabled him to undercut Thomas-Morse's bid and win the job. Boeing also improved on the design, putting engine radiators on the sides of the cockpit instead of on top of the upper wings. The government's order totaled $1.8 million—the company's largest since the end of the war.

The MB-3A put Boeing back into fighting condition, but it still had difficulty selling passenger aircraft, given the market glut. Despite Boeing's attempts to sell seaplanes to local sportsmen, the military—war or no war—was by far its largest customer.

Technological advances continued apace. When the company manufactured 71 NB trainer models for the U.S. Navy, engineers incorporated such progressive features as an air-cooled engine and N-shaped wing struts. Boeing stuck to his pledge to make airplanes of increasing sophistication, continuing to learn from the work of other manufacturers. For example, engineers had studied the construction of the advanced German World War I fighter plane, the Fokker D. VII. They were determined to improve upon the plane, and their revolutionary design, the prototype XPW-9, replaced the Fokker's conventional wood-and-wire fuselage with one welded from steel and braced with piano wire. Instead of the Fokker's wooden wing struts, the XPW-9's wing struts were crafted from steel tubes.

The plane's unique design and top speed of 159 miles per hour brought brisk orders from both the Army and the Navy. Once the plane was out of the experimental stage (hence the "X" in its title), Boeing called it the Model 15, while the Army designated it the PW-9 and the Navy labeled it the FB-1. The planes marked Boeing's first venture manufacturing military fighters of its own design. Between 1923 and 1928, the company built 157 Model 15s in different versions, applying the knowledge it had gleaned in its early years building aircraft and making aircraft systems for competing manufacturers. Later variations included a version made specifically for Navy aircraft carriers with a tailhook that enabled the plane to make controlled landings on a ship—an innovation still used on aircraft carriers today.

The company's growing reputation for developing innovative aircraft soon became its brand identity. As the *Seattle Times* stated in 1920, Boeing planes were "in many respects superior to machines produced by the greatest aircraft factories of the United States."

By the 1920s, several competitors had appeared on the scene and were making planes of equal sophistication. Donald Wills Douglas was among these aviation pioneers. Born in Brooklyn, New York, Douglas reportedly had witnessed early flights by the Wright brothers as a teenager that left an indelible mark. At the United States Naval Academy, where he was enrolled as a cadet, he awed (and perhaps annoyed) his dormitory roommates by making model airplanes with "engines" propelled by rubber bands. Like George Conrad Westervelt, he later studied aeronautical engineering at MIT, and upon graduation he joined several nascent manufacturing entities including Connecticut Aircraft Company and the Glenn Martin Company. In July 1921, he incorporated The Douglas Co.

No sooner had the new venture launched than Douglas landed his first Navy contract to build torpedo bombers, starting with the DT-1. By 1922, the company had delivered six of the aircraft, giving Douglas the financial confidence to lease an abandoned movie studio on Wilshire Boulevard near Santa Monica, California, as a factory. There, the company manufactured the Douglas World

Douglas Aircraft Company built five World Cruisers with the goal of being the first to circumnavigate the globe. Two of the World Cruisers achieved their goal, giving the company its motto, "First Around the World." At right, the company founder, Donald Douglas, stands with a Douglas DT bomber.

Cruiser, a modified version of the DT-2 torpedo bomber, for the sole purpose of doing something no one else had ever done before: circumnavigate the globe by air. The project was financed by the U.S. Army Air Service. Douglas was establishing himself as a tough competitor for the long run.

Four Douglas World Cruisers set off on April 6, 1924, to accomplish what Ferdinand Magellan had achieved four centuries earlier by ship. Douglas had stashed aircraft parts across the globe in case the planes needed repairs en route. Boeing even assisted in the endeavor, its employees in Seattle exchanging the planes' wheels for pontoons for the overwater portion of the flight to Asia. Two of the World Cruisers ultimately made it around the world, logging 27,553 miles in six months and six days (with an actual flying time of 371 hours). The exploit put the company on the map and gave it its motto, "First Around the World."

The following year, James H. "Dutch" Kindelberger joined Douglas Co. as chief engineer. In subsequent years he would lead the development of the famous DC-1 and DC-2 commercial transport aircraft, giving the Douglas Co. a bulwark in the battle for future airline business. Douglas would prove to be one of Boeing's fiercest competitors—and, on occasion, most ardent collaborators.

During this period, Bill Boeing continued to concentrate on making military aircraft rather than passenger planes. A new enterprise soon altered his plans. In 1918, the U.S. Post Office made history by creating the first regularly scheduled airmail service in the United States with a route between Washington, DC, and New York, via an intermediate stop in Philadelphia. The experiment proved the viability of transporting mail by air, and the government inaugurated regular airmail service on May 15, 1919. Six years later, the signing of the U.S. Air Mail Act authorized the U.S. Post Office to award government mail contracts on designated routes to private carriers via a bidding process. Boeing wanted in.

He already had some experience flying the mail. In 1919, he and company pilot Eddie Hubbard flew a Model C-700 biplane carrying 60 letters from Vancouver, British Columbia, to Seattle, marking the first international airmail flight. Back then, Boeing believed the cost of manufacturing planes just to fly the mail was prohibitive. But once airmail service was commercialized, he changed his mind. And he had an idea how to generate an additional source of revenue on the airmail planes: flying passengers.

"A lot of people didn't think it was possible to fly both mail and passengers together," said Bill Boeing Jr. "Boeing airmail was profitable only for one reason—that extra passenger revenue."

A few years later, the company placed its bid for an airmail contract with its new Model 40A plane. It was powered by an air-cooled, 420-hp Pratt & Whitney Wasp engine, which was much lighter than other engines. The plane's low weight permitted the transport of twice the payload, allowing Boeing to tender a lower bid than his competitors.

The company was awarded the contract to deliver airmail between San Francisco and Chicago, and the Model 40A went into service in 1927, two years after its maiden flight. The deal with the government required the manufacture of 26 airplanes in less than a year—a brisk rate of production.

Right: On March 1, 1919, Bill Boeing (standing on the right) and Eddie Hubbard (on the left) flew the first international airmail flight between Seattle and Vancouver, British Columbia.

Far right: Eight years later, the Model 40A became the first Boeing commercial airplane to go into full production.

MAIL
OVER THE RUBY MOU
1773-B

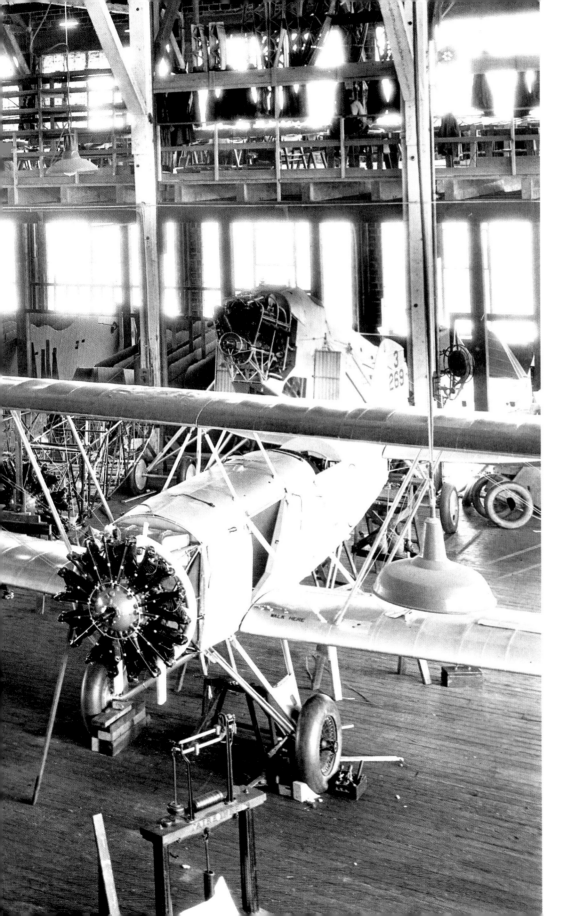

tion. To guarantee it, Boeing had to underwrite a $500,000 bond with his own money.

For the first time, Boeing Airplane Co. would make *and* fly its own planes, piloted by a hired crew. Not only did the Model 40 represent Boeing's first production commercial airplane, it was the beginning of an actual airline.

Boeing Air Transport (BAT), led by Phil Johnson, was formed to run the new airline. At the inauguration of the first BAT airmail flight on July 1, 1927, Bertha Boeing, Bill's wife, performed the traditional champagne bottle–smashing ceremony using orange juice–flavored soda water; champagne was not allowed because Prohibition was in effect. She commented that it "made a satisfactory fizz," but rumors persisted that she had secretly broken the rules and hoisted a bottle of bubbly.

Jane Eads, a reporter for the *Chicago Herald Examiner*, was the first BAT passenger. Elegantly attired in high heels, a knee-length business suit, and a feather boa, she made the 22.5-hour trip between San Francisco and Chicago in a cabin not much bigger than a closet. Bill Boeing had achieved his vision to expand the company's business beyond government contracts, and BAT was the company's first break into commercial aviation. By the end of the year, BAT had transported 1,863 passengers along with 67 tons of mail and other freight. Boeing earned more money than anticipated, and BAT was profitable from its first day of operations.

How important was airmail to the future of the American commercial aviation business? In

Model 40As are shown being put together in Boeing's assembly building on the Duwamish River near Seattle. The small shipyard would witness many advances in early aviation.

a word, vital. "Airmail got commercial flying under way, and it was Boeing that developed the airplane and the system that made flying the mail much cheaper than it had been before," said Brien Wygle, Boeing's former chief test pilot.

In 1928, Boeing Airplane & Transport Company was created as a holding company for both parts of the business—manufacturing and transport. The same year, the holding company purchased control of rival Pacific Air Transport, giving it a virtual lock on all airmail delivered up and down the West Coast, from Los Angeles to Seattle. Shortly thereafter, Boeing and Fred Rentschler, president of Pratt & Whitney Aircraft, a maker of aircraft engines, entered into a stock arrangement to form a new holding company named United Aircraft and Transport Corporation.

With his near-monopoly on West Coast airmail, Bill Boeing now turned his attention to building a plane specifically for passengers: the Model 80 12-passenger biplane. Charles Lindbergh's nonstop transatlantic flight in 1927 had made airplanes seem less dangerous and farfetched as a means of routine transportation. If a plane could travel that far over an ocean with no problems, certainly one could safely transport people from one city to another. Besides, air travel was much faster than other modes of travel, albeit more expensive. The other disadvantages were the rattling, the noise, and the accommodations.

Boeing sought to address these drawbacks in its next plane: the three-engine part-wood, part-metal Model 80. The aircraft was made with passenger comfort in mind and featured leather-upholstered seats and a heated cabin with hot and cold running water. Registered nurses—the world's first female flight attendants—were on board to serve and reassure apprehensive travelers. To stifle the sound of the engines, earplugs were provided to passengers. The plane made its maiden voyage on July 27, 1928, and was quickly put into scheduled service. Sixteen Model 80s were ultimately built, including an upgraded 18-passenger Model 80A in 1930.

The aviation industry was clearly in a growth cycle. From its unassuming beginnings 14 years earlier in a small shipyard building that employees nicknamed the Red Barn, Boeing Airplane Co. had grown to encompass an expanded plant complex comprising 11 buildings equipped with state-of-the-art machinery. With 800 employees on the payroll in 1928, the company was one of the largest aircraft manufacturers in the world.

Bill Boeing at last had found the elusive purpose of his life's work: making increasingly better aircraft. With his company secure, he no longer had to dig into his own wallet to finance the business. The industry's potential seemed as endless as the skies.

The Model 80 biplane (far right) brought passenger air travel into vogue. Registered nurses (right) served as flight attendants and also assisted airsick and nervous passengers.

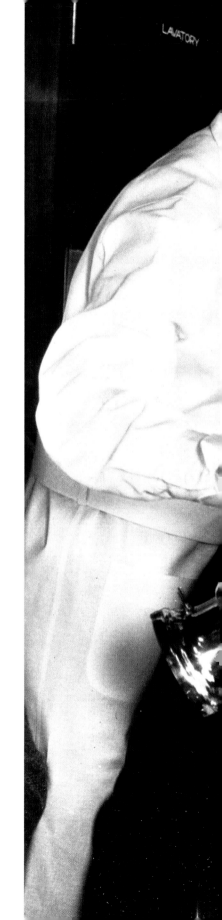

COAT ROOM

12 PASSENGER
217-B

Over the course of 100 years, Boeing has gone from handcrafting small canvas-and-wooden wings for biplanes to producing the high-tech carbon-fiber composite wings of the 787 Dreamliner.

The Age of Aviation

Although the country was in the depths of the worst economic conditions in its history, the prospects for aircraft manufacturing actually increased during the Great Depression. Aviation heroes such as Charles Lindbergh and Amelia Earhart, along with Wiley Post, made headlines by shattering records for altitude, speed, and distance. By the end of the 1930s, air travel was an accepted means of transportation for many people.

The age of aviation had begun, with a fantastic future predicted. *Popular Mechanics* wrote about a "non-stop air express," a massive plane dropping smaller planes from cables for departing passengers. *Popular Science* predicted that huge "islands of ice" would soon dot the oceans as airport hubs. Even Henry Ford, whose Model T car had made automobiles affordable for the masses, forecast an airplane in every garage—"air flivvers," he called them.

Despite the continuing economic crisis, United Aircraft and Transport invested in this future by adding marquee names to its roster of airframe manufacturers, engine makers, and airlines, including Sikorsky, Stout Airlines, and National Air Transport. The company grouped the airlines under one name: United Air Lines, the precursor of today's United Airlines. "What [Bill Boeing] was imagining very early on was the modern corporation," author Clive Irving said. "He saw that you had to put all those bits together." This combined control of supply, production, and distribution— what is known today as vertical integration—was increasingly part of the company's success.

By 1933, United Aircraft and Transport was a vast enterprise. It transported roughly half of all the passengers and airmail in the United States. It manufactured aircraft and components. It even managed airports, including the United Airport in Burbank, California, which touted the world's "first million-dollar terminal." It also founded the Boeing School of Aeronautics in Oakland, California, to train the pilots needed to fly its planes and the mechanics to maintain their reliable operation.

The company was the industry's frontrunner, but there was growing competition from other pioneering aviation concerns led by men who were determined to build market share.

Among them was Jack Northrop, who began his career as a draftsman-engineer for Loughead (later changed to Lockheed) Aircraft Manufacturing Company but left to work at Douglas Aircraft in 1923. Four years later, he assisted Jack Ryan of Ryan Aircraft in designing the larger wing of Lindbergh's *Spirit of St. Louis* plane. In 1932, Northrop, with financial backing from Donald Douglas, incorporated a new enterprise called Northrop Corporation in El Segundo, California. The company manufactured several successful monoplanes, planes with a single set of wings instead of the biplane's two. There was a distinct advantage to a single wing set: the external struts and cables needed to support the weight of earlier aircraft could be eliminated, and the surface area could be reduced by half. Both the weight and the drag produced by the aircraft declined considerably, enabling greater speed and distance. Northrop's *Gamma* monoplane broke world speed records and recorded the first flight across the Antarctic.

Dutch Kindelberger left his position as vice president of engineering at Douglas Aircraft to become the president of North American Aviation in 1934. Founded six years earlier, North American initially was a holding company like United Aircraft

Previous spread: The luxurious Douglas DC-3 is recognized as the greatest airliner of its time.

Left and right: The Boeing Model 200 Monomail helped make biplanes a thing of the past.

and Transport Corp., comprising multiple airlines and aircraft-manufacturing businesses. Two former designers from Douglas, Lee Atwood and Stan Smithson, joined Kindelberger at his request. North American's first government contract was for 161 sets of pontoons for Navy observation planes. An order for 42 NA-16 trainers soon followed. Later, Kindelberger was put in charge of the manufacturing business at the company's new Los Angeles headquarters.

Like Bill Boeing, James Smith McDonnell, who founded J.S. McDonnell & Associates in 1928, was a pilot. His first aircraft, the *Doodlebug*, a tandem-seat monoplane, crashed in a 1929 flight competition, nearly killing him. As the Great Depression took hold, he was forced to dissolve the company and found work first as a consulting engineer and test pilot and later at Martin Aircraft. After raising $165,000, he again entered the manufacturing business, incorporating McDonnell Aircraft Corp. in 1939. He rented office space at the Park Plaza Hotel in St. Louis, Missouri, and recruited a small engineering team. The first year of business produced a loss, and the company struggled until World War II put it on firmer footing.

The celebrated pilot and social gadabout Howard Hughes inherited his father's thriving Hughes Tool Company at a young age and successfully expanded and diversified his holdings to amass great wealth. The brash Hughes produced aviator movies including *Hell's Angels*, dated well-known actresses including Katharine Hepburn, and created a few spectacular airplanes. In 1932, he founded Hughes Aircraft Company in Glendale, California. It manufactured the H-1 racer, a wood-and-metal single-seat monoplane. Hughes was at the controls of the H-1 when it earned a world landplane speed record of 352 miles per hour in 1935.

Like Dutch Kindelberger and Bill Boeing, Hughes vertically integrated his aviation enterprises. In addition to building airplane prototypes,

in 1939, he acquired 77 percent of Transcontinental & Western Air. TWA was one of the Big Four American airlines that also included Eastern Air Lines, United Air Lines, and American Airlines. The airline operated a major transcontinental route from New York to Los Angeles.

As the new companies fought to gain a foothold in the burgeoning industry, their heated battles for airline and government orders led to an extraordinary array of aviation innovations. Chief among these were the transition from wooden components to metal parts and the migration from biplanes to monoplanes. Each product introduced was quickly outdone by a competitor's product.

At Boeing, the all-metal Monomail, a monoplane that carried airmail, featured the industry's first practical retractable landing gear. Designed by Claire Egtvedt and Boeing chief engineer Monty Monteith, its single metal wing was set lower on the fuselage than on Douglas Aircraft's planes. Also featuring a streamlined fuselage and an engine enclosed in an anti-drag cowling, the Monomail was the most advanced, aerodynamic, and cost-efficient commercial airplane in the industry in 1930—until another Boeing plane bested it.

No sooner had the Monomail gone into service than its successor, the Model 247 airliner, was ready for production. Aviation experts consider the Model 247 to be the first truly modern commercial airliner. The aircraft incorporated multiple firsts, including variable pitch propellers, wing deicers, trim tabs, and an autopilot. Boeing also unveiled a bevy of new passenger comforts, including a heated cabin, individual reading lights, toilets, and a galley. The innovative plane leap-frogged competitors' planes with these modern developments. So advanced was the Model 247 that it was a star of the Chicago World's Fair in 1933, which was named "The Century of Progress." The plane regularly took off and landed at the fair, to the delight of spectators.

Unfortunately, on a transcontinental flight the same year, a 247 was destroyed by an explosive device that had been planted on the plane. All aboard died, including three crew members and four passengers. A subsequent federal investigation was unable to pinpoint a suspect, and the case remains unsolved.

But it was not this disaster that spelled doom for the 247. It was Boeing's refusal to provide planes to other airlines until the first 60 were delivered to Boeing's United Air Lines. TWA wanted to purchase several 247s, but Boeing's board of directors declined to squeeze it into the queue ahead of United Air Lines. So TWA sent out a request for bids to competing manufacturers, and Douglas won the business with its twin-engine DC-1.

Douglas's success demonstrated the value of a second-to-market strategy—patiently waiting for a competitor's plane to make its debut and then quickly incorporating and improving upon its new features. This continuous process of adaptation fostered many technological advancements that otherwise might have taken more years to materialize.

The DC-1's success cost Boeing dearly. In subsequent years, the aircraft was refined into the legendary DC-3, a plane significantly larger and faster than the Model 247. Introduced in 1936, the DC-3 had what airlines wanted: a cabin that accommodated 21 passengers (compared to 10 on the 247), a 1,500-mile range, and two reliable 1,200-hp Twin Wasp Pratt & Whitney engines.

Donald Douglas knew he had a winner. Although remembered as a quiet, introspective, and reflective leader, he promoted the plane skillfully.

A Boeing Model 247D flies over New York. The all-metal, twin-engine aircraft is considered the first modern passenger plane.

When Inter-Island Airways (the modern Hawaiian Airlines) ordered three DC-3s, he agreed to a bold idea offered by Inter-Island's founder, Stanley Kennedy Sr.—to have the planes fly 2,500 miles across the Pacific Ocean from Oakland, California, to Honolulu for delivery. To accommodate the additional 1,000-mile distance, the seats inside the planes were removed and replaced with spare fuel tanks and oil drums. Thousands of spectators were in attendance as the DC-3s arrived over Waikiki Beach.

More than 15,000 DC-3 airliners in civilian and military versions were ultimately manufactured through 1946. By comparison, Boeing built 74 Model 247s. So revolutionary was the DC-3 that in 2014, 78 years after its debut, it is still safely flying passengers and freight with airlines across the globe. The legendary aircraft took the wind out of Boeing's sails. Boeing Airplane Company's head start making passenger planes lost all momentum.

The bruising competition from the Douglas DC series was not the worst news for Boeing in the mid-1930s. Even in the collapsed economy, the airmail business was a gold mine for the aviation industry. Newspapers caught wind of the airlines' profits and soon alleged that the industry had engaged in collusion to reap higher government subsidies. A controversial Congressional investigation was launched, in which Boeing and his peers were accused of getting rich off the backs of taxpayers. When the investigation concluded, the federal government acted swiftly. It passed the Air Mail Act of 1934, which forced holding companies to separate aircraft manufacturing from their airline operations. In effect, aircraft manufacturers could no longer own mail-carrying airlines. The industry's vertical integration strategy came to an abrupt halt.

United Aircraft and Transport was split into three independent entities: United Air Lines (responsible for air transportation), Boeing Airplane

Co. (responsible for manufacturing operations), and United Aircraft (responsible for manufacturing operations in the eastern United States and later renamed United Technologies). United Aircraft comprised several previous acquisitions such as Sikorsky and Pratt & Whitney.

For Bill Boeing, the breakup of his company was an insult to his integrity and vision. He had long contended that the capital influx from airmail contracts served the public because it was reinvested in aviation advancements. In later years, he would say that the government's hasty decision had curtailed the industry's progress by half.

The industry's former airmail contracts were turned over to the U.S. Army Air Corps, which was unprepared for the responsibility. The Air Corps suffered numerous crashes and fatalities by pilots untrained for bad weather conditions. With the public in an uproar, President Franklin Roosevelt had no choice but to return service to the commercial airlines. In 1941, the U.S. Court of Claims would rule that there had been no fraud or collusion in the awarding of airmail contracts. Boeing and the other pioneers of commercial aviation were absolved of any misconduct.

Bill Boeing had founded a company that was in the process of changing the world, and the government broke it up—as it turned out, based on false suppositions. But the vindication came too late for him. In 1934, following the industry's breakup, Boeing resigned as chairman. His vision of the company suppressed by the government's decision, Boeing sold his stock and for the rest of his life observed the company that bore his name

from the sidelines. He pursued a quiet retirement in the Pacific Northwest, raising Thoroughbred horses, sailing the *Taconite,* and keeping his pilot's license active.

The loss of Bill Boeing was an unexpected setback, made worse by the fact that business prospects had again fallen off. Claire Egtvedt assumed the chairman's position and continued in his duties as president, a post he had filled since 1933. The gifted former mechanical engineer had been in charge of all aircraft engineering since 1917 and had been responsible for numerous technological enhancements through the years. His steady hand was needed as even more turbulent times lay ahead.

War was again brewing in Europe. Adolf Hitler had assumed power in Germany and rearmed the military. Hitler's aggressive actions indicated a growing need for modern military equipment in Europe and the United States. In particular focus was the manufacture of large aircraft able to transport weaponry and personnel—the aerial equivalent of battleships.

Egtvedt believed the company's best prospects were to design and make extremely large bombers. Such giant planes represented a major departure for Boeing, as the company was known primarily as a manufacturer of small fighter planes. In retrospect, had Egtvedt not redirected the company toward large bombers, the future could have turned out much differently for Boeing. Its expertise in these airplanes would play an important role in its later development of passenger jetliners.

Douglas Aircraft developed the DC-1 in response to Boeing's 247. Only one was built (far left), but the company quickly followed up with the DC-2 (left). The DC-3 would go on to become one of the best-selling planes in history, and still flies today.

Egtvedt wanted the bomber's design to share features with a large airliner—a two-for-one market strategy. Boeing engineers led by Jack Klystra responded with the experimental XB-15, the largest and heaviest plane ever built at the time. The XB-15 boasted a wingspan of 149 feet—so immense that the crew could venture through passageways in the wings to make minor repairs while the plane was in the air.

The XB-15 was designed to achieve the Army Air Corps' plans for a heavy bomber that could achieve a range of 5,000 miles. For a company that had previously manufactured small airplanes, this was a completely new Boeing.

The experimental plane, the very first of the "big Boeings," set the foundation for larger, more powerful, and much faster aircraft in the years ahead. The first of these planes was the Model 299, later known as the B-17 bomber, which boasted an almost 74-foot length and a wingspan of more than 103 feet. Looking at the 22-ton plane armed with an array of machine guns and a 4,000-pound bomb load, a newsman remarked, "It's a flying fortress." The name stuck.

The Army Air Corps was looking to purchase 200 long-range bombers. In competition with Douglas and Martin, Boeing submitted the prototype for the B-17 but failed to win the contract when the plane crashed, killing two of the five crewmen on board. Its vast size also was a concern to a few high-ranking military officers who feared it would be a bull's-eye in the sky. Nevertheless, the Air Corps was impressed by the plane's design and ordered 13 B-17s for further evaluation. To build them, Boeing constructed a second plant, Plant 2, on 28 acres two miles south of its first plant and doubled the total work-

force to 1,500 employees by 1939. "It is a considerable source of pride that we are producing the most advanced type of defensive aircraft ever offered our country," *Boeing News* reported.

As Egtvedt had planned, the XB-15 also gave birth to a commercial airliner, the Model 314 Clipper seaplane. Like its sibling, the B-17, the Model 314 was gigantic. It weighed 82,000 pounds, was 106 feet long from nose to tail, and could transport 74 passengers over a distance of 3,500 miles—far enough to cross the Atlantic or parts of the Pacific. It was the jumbo jet of its day.

The Clipper was built specifically for Pan American Airways, founded by Juan Trippe. When he was a boy, Trippe witnessed Wilbur Wright's 1909 flight around the Statue of Liberty; after getting his pilot's license and graduating from Yale University, he incorporated an airline, Aviation Corporation of the Americas, which evolved into Pan American Airways in 1927.

Trippe wanted a first-class aircraft that could speed passengers to exotic destinations in unheard-of luxury. Boeing's Model 314 Clipper—named for the fast sailing ships of the 19th century because it took off from and landed on water—fit the bill. It boasted an elegant dining room and bar, dressing rooms for men and women, seats that faced each other so passengers could converse or play cards, and even a bridal suite for newlyweds. "[The Clipper was] beautiful, silver-hulled, and very majestic, all this glamor happening during the midst of the Great Depression," said Yale University history professor Jenifer Van Vleck.

Service from San Francisco to Singapore commenced in March 1939, and transatlantic runs were inaugurated with the Atlantic Clipper that June, allowing regular air service between the United States and Britain.

The same year, Boeing's four-engine Model 307 Stratoliner made its debut. Once again, Boeing moved the industry forward, continuing to develop

The Boeing Model 314 Clipper (right and far right) was renowned for its luxury. The plane featured dressing rooms, sleeping berths, lounges, and even a honeymoon suite.

The largest passenger plane of its time, the Model 314 seaplane was called the Clipper, a nod to the fast, long-distance sailing ships of the previous century.

innovative designs inspired by the success of existing aircraft. In the aviation industry, this process is referred to today as "adaptive architecture." Boeing learned from its success with the XB-15 to create both the Clipper and the B-17. Now the B-17 would inform the development of the Model 307, combining the former plane's wings, tail, rudder, landing gear, and engines with a revolutionary fuselage that could be pressurized.

The Stratoliner thus became the first commercial airliner to enter service with a pressurized cabin. This allowed the plane to soar above storm-induced turbulence at altitudes of 20,000 feet, approximately two-thirds the height of Mount Everest. Before this historic achievement, flying above 12,500 feet caused passenger discomfort and oxygen deprivation due to the low outside air pressure. Flight attendants, all of them registered nurses, conveyed oxygen bottles attached to masks to give the beleaguered passengers a breath of air.

It is hard to fathom just how uncomfortable air travel was in the 1930s. Boeing flight attendants frequently spent their time treating travelers experiencing motion sickness from the aircraft's constant jostling and turbulence at lower altitudes. If the pilot flew the plane higher, passengers had trouble breathing in the thinner air.

Both Boeing and Douglas had experimented with air pressurization, pumping conditioned air into the cabin at high altitudes to maintain the air pressure of a lower altitude. Thanks to ventilation expert Nate Price, Boeing broke the tape first. Price's patent called for the Model 307 Stratoliner to ascend, unpressurized, to 8,000

feet, a level where passengers could breathe normally. Above this level, a supercharger on each of the inboard engines pumped air in from outside the plane to maintain air pressure in the cabin. Above 16,000 feet, where the air was even thinner, cabin pressure diminished slightly. But at 20,000 feet, the plane was above the worst of the weather, allowing normal breathing, reducing motion sickness, and enabling the plane to fly a more direct route. Although Boeing sold only 74 Stratoliners (and produced just 10, as Boeing turned all of its resources to building B-17s for the war effort), its technological ingenuity contributed immensely to the future comfort of all passenger aircraft.

In the space of a decade, air travel had transformed from a sole human being flying across the Atlantic to the cheers of an astonished public to anyone with the price of a ticket regularly and comfortably doing the same. Companies in the growing industry outdid each other with advanced design and manufacturing concepts, producing ever faster, larger, and more sophisticated aircraft. This continuous improvement process soon became the norm.

For Boeing—shaken by the Air Mail Act of 1934 and the abrupt resignation of its founder—new president Claire Egtvedt's reimagining of the company as a maker of large, long-range airplanes came just in time. With the fuse ignited by Germany's continuing aggression, another world war would soon explode in Europe. Egtvedt's belief in the value of big bombers would prove crucial to the future of the industry and the fate of the free world.

Although only 10 Model 307 Stratoliners were built (left), the passenger plane ushered in a new era of passenger comfort, with a pressurization system that enabled it to fly above bad weather, and plush seats that converted to sleeping berths (right).

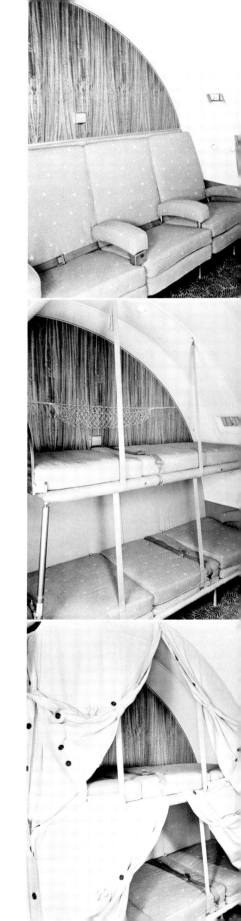

The name of the 787 Dreamliner (right) was chosen in a worldwide vote and echoes the name of another game-changing Boeing passenger plane—the 307 Stratoliner (left).

The Arsenal of Democracy

By 1940, Germany had established a massive military operation in Europe. A prominent component of its armed forces was the Luftwaffe. This modern air force, composed of some of the most advanced aircraft ever manufactured, was dedicated primarily to tactical bombing in support of the German army's blitzkrieg operations. Its directives were to bomb enemy bases, strike enemy ground troops, and destroy roads, bridges, tunnels, and railways.

One by one, the countries of the Continent fell to the Third Reich—Czechoslovakia, Poland, Denmark, Norway, Holland, Belgium, and France. If Great Britain were conquered, Adolf Hitler could take control of its Royal Navy. Were this to happen, many U.S. government officials feared, Hitler could easily land his army divisions on the Eastern Seaboard of the United States.

The American public remained steadfast that they did not want the country to engage in another war. But with Britain threatened, on December 29, 1940, President Franklin D. Roosevelt gave an urgent address to American industry and the public at large. "Our national policy is not directed toward war [but] it is the purpose of the nation to build now with all possible speed every machine, every arsenal, every factory that we need to manufacture our defense material," Roosevelt stated. "We must be the great arsenal of democracy."

The president appealed to all U.S. manufacturers to unite their industries toward arming the Allies in Europe and the military forces at home. The government would immediately fund these efforts, with the largest portion of the spending (32 percent) earmarked for the manufacture of aircraft. Although an attack by sea was considered a higher risk, Roosevelt was concerned that Luftwaffe aircraft traveling 300 miles per hour could potentially traverse the ocean to bomb U.S. targets. At the time, the U.S. Army Air Corps had a mere 1,200 planes. The president proposed to Congress that the country develop "the ability to turn out at least 50,000 planes a year."

The president was essentially asking Boeing and its rivals to cooperate with each other by sharing their technology and building each other's planes. They obliged, breaking down competitive barriers and joining forces on the mass production of military aircraft. As the major aircraft manufacturers retooled their production capabilities on behalf of the country, profound technological advancements resulted from their teamwork.

Government orders were brisk and shockingly large—more than 12,000 B-17 Flying Fortresses were ultimately purchased. "The B-17 was a miracle plane as far as the Air Force was concerned," said World War II historian Donald Miller. "It was faster. It was sturdier. And it had more firepower than anything that the Air Force had envisioned."

The bomber's design provided substantial bomb load capacity, as much as 8,000 pounds, although the average was 4,000 to 5,000 pounds per trip. The plane featured as many as 13 machine guns, depending on the model; .50-caliber waist and tail guns; one gun turret under the fuselage and another on top of the plane behind the cockpit; and advanced protective armor, including self-sealing fuel tanks. With a speed surpassing 300 miles per hour and a range of 2,000 miles, the B-17 could deeply penetrate enemy territory and accurately attack enemy military and industrial targets. It was made to take a beating in the skies and make it back home safely. To the U.S. military, it was perceived as indispensable.

Previous spread: When World War II broke out, demands for military airplanes led to an unprecedented ramp-up in production for all American aviation companies.

Left and right: The B-17 Flying Fortress was legendary for its toughness and stability.

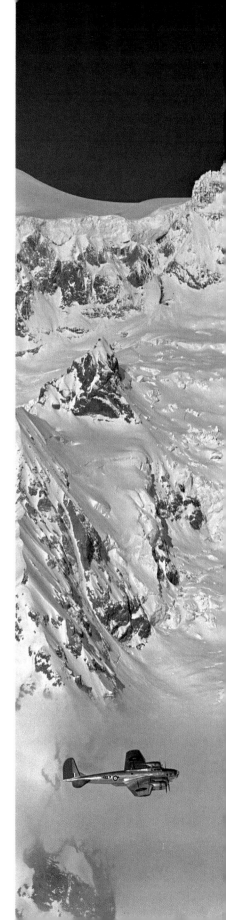

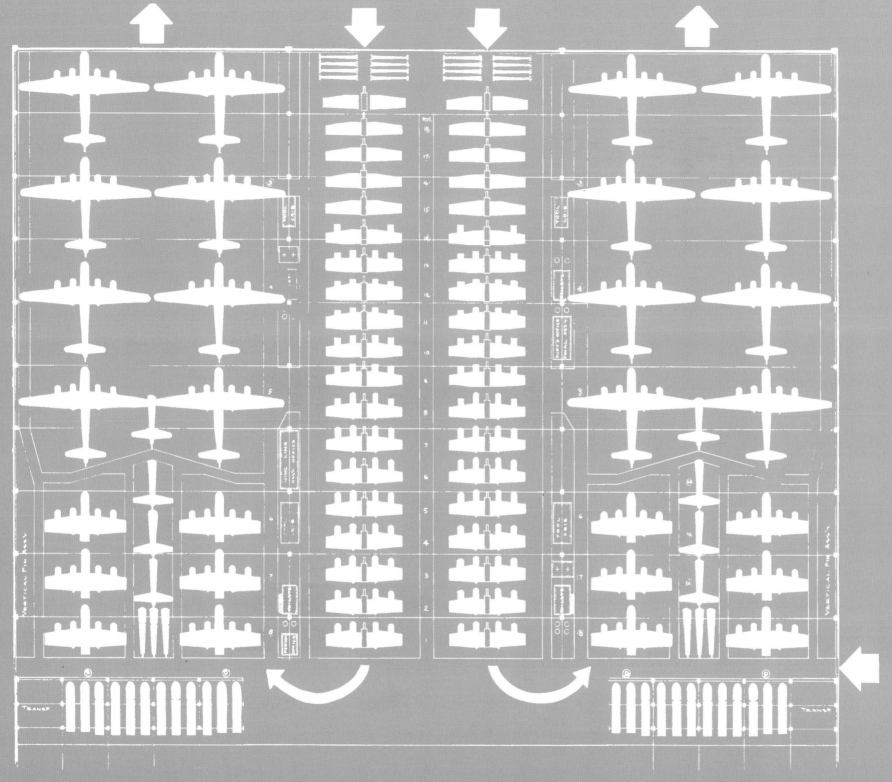

A B-29 factory production layout (left) and view of the factory floor (right) show just how efficient and fast-paced production of the B-17 and B-29 was. More than 10,000 B-17s were built by Boeing and its partners over the course of the war.

But building thousands of planes in just months? To succeed, Boeing and its competitors—Douglas, North American Aviation, McDonnell, Hughes, Lockheed, and others—became a single unit, a powerhouse of manufacturing expertise, resources, and output. Planes were no longer made one at a time. Modern factories sprang from the ground across the country, their assembly lines rolling out sophisticated aircraft at unprecedented rates.

When the United States entered the war in 1941, many young Americans were either soldiers or factory workers. Around-the-clock production was in force with 24-hour days and three shifts of workers. Some workers slept at the factory between shifts. With so many men fighting the war, women were recruited to work at the factories. While their husbands and fathers were overseas, these women—collectively nicknamed "Rosie the Riveter"—pulled double shifts, working at the plant building airplanes and then doing domestic chores at home. To assist them, Boeing created a transportation department that organized ride sharing and busing, helped working mothers obtain day care for their children, and provided flexible work shifts so mothers could work at night and be home during the day with their kids. By war's end, one out of three factory workers in America was a woman.

With the war in full swing, the entire aviation industry went to work. Boeing built the B-17 Flying Fortress at Plant 2 in Seattle. Douglas and Lockheed also built the vital bomber. Due to the extraordinary importance of warplane manufacture, conditions in Seattle were akin to martial law. The

With so many men away fighting in the war, women, known collectively as Rosie the Riveter, replaced them in the aviation factories. By the end of the war, more than 40 percent of Boeing's workforce was female.

government imposed periodic blackouts, and after sunset, drivers to and from the Boeing plant could use only their parking lights, no headlights. The rooftop of the facility was camouflaged with burlap and chicken wire to look from the sky like a residential neighborhood.

Wartime demands changed Seattle from a remote outpost in the Pacific Northwest into a sprawling hub of activity. Boeing and the city's shipyards hired tens of thousands of employees, and housing developments popped up like mushrooms to lodge them. Employment at the company climbed sharply from about 9,920 workers in 1940 to some 78,400 in 1943.

In addition to building the Flying Fortress, the company started churning out B-29 Superfortress heavy bombers. The four-engine Superfortress was the most complex airplane to be built until that time, a triumph in both design and performance. Nearly 100 feet long, the Superfortress weighed more than 105,000 pounds, making it the heaviest production aircraft in the world. Its innovations included a formidable armament with remote-controlled gun turrets. It was the first strategic bomber equipped with a pressurized cabin, which enabled pilots and crew to fly long distances—a necessity in the vast Pacific theater.

The Superfortress was the largest single airplane production program during the war, an industrial project of a size and scale that American industry had never before experienced. It encompassed a nationwide network of manufacturing plants as well as hundreds of subcontractors.

During the war, key manufacturing plants were camouflaged to prevent them from being targeted by enemy airplanes. From the air, Boeing Plant 2 looked like a suburban neighborhood.

General Henry "Hap" Arnold, commanding general of the U.S. Army Air Forces, wanted the B-29 ready by March 1944—an extremely ambitious objective for engineers and production personnel. To help achieve it, Boeing's plant in Wichita—formerly a Stearman Aircraft facility that was also busy producing Kaydet primary trainers—waged the "Battle of Kansas." Area farmhands, housewives, and shopkeepers worked grueling 10-hour shifts in the bitter cold, day and night, to manufacture the first 175 "Superforts," as they called them.

The hard work paid off: because of its long range, the B-29 became the primary bomber used against Japan. In Europe, meanwhile, thousands of B-17s attacked land-based targets from the sky, dropping more than 640,000 tons of bombs in all, more than any other military plane.

While Boeing worked primarily on the B-17 and B-29, each aviation company did its part, drawing from its particular expertise to produce military planes in concert with other manufacturers.

Dutch Kindelberger's North American Aviation was a powerhouse of production, building 41,000 planes for the war effort. During peak production, an airplane rolled off its assembly lines every 15 minutes.

Among the planes manufactured by North American was the AT-6 trainer, which was invaluable given the immediate need to instruct thousands of new pilots. The trainers were manufactured at its sprawling plant in Dallas—hence the plane's name, the Texan, although it was called the Harvard outside the United States.

North American Aviation also made the B-25 Mitchell twin-engine medium bomber named for

Right: The B-29 is widely considered the most technologically advanced bomber mass-produced during World War II. It first flew September 21, 1942.

General Billy Mitchell, an airpower pioneer. The B-25B was the first bomber deployed in all World War II combat theaters and the first American bomber to sink Axis submarines. Most famously, the B-25 was involved in the sneak air attack on Japan known as the Doolittle Raid. In April 1942, under the command of Lieutenant Colonel Jimmy Doolittle, 16 Mitchell medium bombers, each crewed by five men, took off without fighter escort from the deck of the USS *Hornet* aircraft carrier, which was stationed in the western Pacific Ocean. The plan called for the planes to bomb multiple military targets in Japan and then continue westward to land in China. Despite flying a longer distance than anticipated and with less fuel than was thought needed to make it to the prearranged landing fields in China, the B-25s nonetheless made their strikes, dropping bombs "as easily as a political speech to a Congressman," the *Seattle Times* reported in 1942.

Fifteen of the aircraft got as far as China; the other one landed in Vladivostok, Russia. Although the raid did little to damage Japan's military clout, the country was forced to keep back large numbers of fighter aircraft to defend itself, leaving fewer available to fight U.S. forces above the Pacific islands. More important, the attack on Japan's home territory was a psychological blow. At the same time, it boosted U.S. confidence and morale, accelerating the commitment to win the war through American ingenuity.

Of all its warplanes, North American's P-51 Mustang fighter stands out. Unlike other military aircraft such as bombers and attack planes, fighters are designed primarily for air-to-air combat.

The sleek, long-range, single-seat P-51 fighter boasted exceptional maneuverability and speed. It also was highly reliable and had the range to escort the heavy bombers all the way to their targets, defending them from airborne attack. Powered by a Rolls-Royce Merlin engine, the Mustang was faster and more dangerous than the Luftwaffe's prized Messerschmitt fighters. When reports about the superior plane reached Nazi Air Minister Hermann Goering, he is reported to have said, "We have lost the war."

Douglas Aircraft also stepped up its game. Donald Douglas had vowed "to build the largest number possible of the best airplanes in the shortest possible time." Workers made good on his pledge, producing 29,385 warplanes from 1941 to 1944, roughly 16 percent of all the U.S. warplanes manufactured during the war.

Douglas Aircraft's most important wartime plane was the C-47, developed from the DC-3 airliner. More than 10,000 C-47s were built. Douglas had to build new factories to accommodate the robust production, including a 1.4-million-square-foot plant in Long Beach, California, camouflaged with trees and shrubs. At its peak, the massive plant rolled out one airplane each hour.

Hughes Aircraft Co. and McDonnell Aircraft served during the war primarily as subcontractors. Hughes Aircraft's diverse contracts ran the gamut from wings to rear fuselage sections. Other Hughes companies manufactured large quantities of aircraft ammunition belts during the war.

McDonnell manufactured aircraft parts such as tails and engine cowlings for both Boeing bombers and Douglas transports—seven million pounds of aircraft parts in all. Its single contract with the U.S. Army Air Forces was for an experimental prototype, the XP-67, a novel twin-engine, long-range fighter with a pressurized cockpit. The company also was awarded a contract to build the first jet-propelled Navy fighter, the XFD-1, but the war ended before it could go into production.

Crews conduct an engine test on a B-25 Mitchell bomber (far left). North American Aviation built almost 10,000 of the planes during World War II.

The military derivative of the DC-3 was known as the C-47 Skytrain (left). It was used to transport troops and cargo throughout the war.

In succeeding years, this plane would evolve into the historic FH-1 Phantom fighter, the first American jet that could operate from an aircraft carrier. The FH-1, which had a top speed of 500 miles per hour, was an audacious achievement given the thrust needed by such a heavy aircraft to take off from a flight deck and the seeming impossibility of landing on the same stunted airstrip.

The Phantom made its first carrier takeoff and landing in July 1945. "I remember seeing films of the first takeoff from the carrier and the first landing," said John McDonnell, the founder's son. "Everybody was pretty tense"—no one more than the pilot, he added. "In terms of heart rate, I've heard [it's] higher than it is in combat." Although only 62 FH-1 Phantoms were built, the jet was the beginning of a long line of McDonnell jet fighters whose success would define the company in the second half of the 20th century.

While U.S. and European aircraft manufacturers collaborated in the production of warplanes, one company took the lead in organizing the industry and its army of subcontractors in the unmatched production effort: Boeing. Phil Johnson, the company's president (Egtvedt remained chairman), was in charge of the industry's warplane manufacture—a Herculean task. The vast number of warplanes wanted by the government required an unheard-of level of coordination within the aviation industry to manufacture the required components—from airframes to engines, control systems, and varying armaments—in specific and short time frames.

The merciless pace of wartime production likely contributed to the stroke that led to Johnson's death in 1944, an event mourned by factory workers, generals, and presidents. By then, he had built the foundation underpinning President Roosevelt's objective of producing 50,000 warplanes a year, a volume initially believed impossible. The industry went further, manufacturing a staggering 96,000 warplanes a year. Gradually, the Axis war industry was hobbled, thanks in no small part to the B-17 and the B-29. "In combat, Boeing's two Fortresses were unexcelled," *Time* magazine stated in 1954.

The planes also lived up to their reputation for being able to take a beating and return home safely. One legendary story involved a midair collision between a B-17, the *All American*, and a German fighter above Tunisia in 1943. The fighter came apart, its pieces piercing the B-17. The four-engine bomber's left horizontal stabilizer and left elevator were torn off in the collision. The two right engines were knocked out of commission, one of the left engines leaked oil, the vertical fin and the rudder were badly damaged, and the torn fuselage was held together at only two small junctures. Despite a cavernous 16-foot-long hole in the fuselage and damage to the plane's radios and electrical and oxygen systems, the Flying Fortress landed safely two and a half hours after the collision. The entire crew survived.

As the war in Europe drew to a close following the surrender of Germany on May 7, 1945, battles still continued in the Pacific theater. Boeing's long-range B-29 Superfortress was called upon for one last task: dropping atomic bombs on Japan. Colonel Paul Tibbetts released the atomic bomb on Hiroshima from a plane named the *Enola Gay*. Three days later, a second B-29, the *Bockscar*, dropped a bomb on Nagasaki, the last nuclear attack in history. The Second World War ended on August 14, 1945, and air power had determined its outcome.

Boeing, Douglas, McDonnell, North American, and Hughes—the companies that constitute the modern Boeing—had helped achieve victory for Allied forces while serving as a powerful symbol

North American Aviation built more than 15,000 P-51 Mustang fighters. The P-51D Mustang (right and far right) was arguably the best fighter plane of the Second World War.

of American ingenuity, productivity, and might. Their willingness to share secret technologies, the cross-cultivation of their skill sets, and Boeing's ability to act as the master contractor overseeing a colossal production effort set the stage for more complex and innovative aircraft. Each company emerged from the war with defined talents, which would foster industry specialization in the years ahead. The war won and their years of collaboration now concluded, the major builders of the arsenal of democracy returned to the free market.

A B-29 Superfortress was named for Ernie Pyle shortly following the death of the beloved war correspondent.

Military aviation has changed dramatically since World War II, but research and development are still key to success. A model of the B-17 is tested in Boeing's war-era wind tunnel (left); more than 65 years later, a Phantom Ray unmanned vehicle prototype, developed by Boeing Phantom Works, receives a preflight inspection.

Postwar Innovation

The satisfaction of knowing that Boeing's long-range heavy bombers had brought closure to the war was immediately supplanted by mounting uncertainty over the company's future. The postwar years boomed for many U.S. industries, less at first for the aviation business. A few weeks after the war's official end, employees at Boeing plants from Seattle to Wichita received the bad news: all company factories would be shut down. The year had begun with nearly 70,000 employees; 9,000 remained.

The same day many Boeing plants stopped production—September 1, 1945—a new president was appointed by the board of directors. William M. "Bill" Allen, a lawyer originally from tiny Lolo, Montana, had his work cut out for him. As *Nation's Business* reported, "World War II was over, and Boeing, except for a few small jobs, was out of business." Sales that had totaled nearly $421 million in 1945 dropped to $13 million in 1946. "Profits turned to losses," the magazine added. "But, Bill Allen didn't panic."

It was Allen's nature to remain calm in times of duress. He had been a Boeing board director and its chief legal counsel for 15 years prior to assuming the presidency two years after Phil Johnson's death (the post had gone unfilled in the meantime). Allen regularly understated his importance and even tried to convince Boeing's board that he was the wrong man for the job. On that score, he was completely wrong. As *Time* magazine stated in 1954, "He was no airman, but he knew Boeing's finances inside out."

Given the company's ominous financial shape, such knowledge was required. But it was even more important for Allen and his team to strategically determine the types of aircraft the military and commercial airlines would want to buy. Many technological breakthroughs had been realized by the industry through its joint enterprises during the war. When Boeing and the other companies returned to competitive market conditions, all built

upon their collective technological achievements to design and develop more advanced aircraft on their own.

With military orders a fraction of their wartime volume, Boeing's focus shifted to commercial airliners, a market that had been static during the war. Building on the company's developments in military aircraft, Allen directed the manufacture of a luxurious commercial version of the four-engine C-97 military freighter, which itself was a derivative of the B-29 Superfortress. The commercial variant was introduced to the market as the Boeing Model 377 Stratocruiser. When the Stratocruiser entered scheduled transatlantic service from New York to London in 1949, passengers were provided foldaway sleeper berths, gilded dressing rooms, and seats with a button to signal the stewardess. A staircase led from the main cabin, which seated four abreast, to a lounge below able to accommodate 14 passengers.

The double-decker plane was extolled in advertisements as the "new queen of the skies"—the former queen being Boeing's 1930s-era Clipper. "Cocktails and delicious full-course meals, prepared in flight, are served with our compliments," ads promised.

Despite its elegance and Allen's high hopes, the plane was not a financial success. Chief rival Douglas Aircraft Company returned to prewar form with a new plane in the DC series, the DC-6. The airplane's four Pratt & Whitney engines delivered twice the power of those used on the wartime DC-4, and the cost to buy and operate it was less than that of the Model 377. While the major airlines bought both planes and Boeing was able for the first time to make significant progress selling its aircraft to foreign airlines, the DC-6 was preferred—by far. Douglas sold 700 DC-6s; Boeing a comparatively paltry 56 Stratocruisers.

But in typical Boeing style, even as the Stratocruiser faltered, the company continued to invest in research and development. With the company's typical instinct for making the right call at the right time—and some luck—it found its footing in the most dramatic of ways.

The stunning turnabout in the commercial airliner market had all the trappings of a great adventure tale. As World War II wound down, General Henry "Hap" Arnold, commanding general of the U.S. Army Air Forces, assembled a team of scientists and engineers to undertake a highly covert operation. The project was called Luftwaffe Secret Technology, nicknamed Operation LUSTY, and the team's goal was to hunt for German aviation technology. General Arnold appointed Theodore von Karman, a Hungarian-born scientist, to lead the team.

Von Karman had escaped Germany as the Nazis came into power, and he became a naturalized American citizen. When Arnold contacted him, he was the director of the Guggenheim Aeronautical Laboratory at the California Institute of Technology. Von Karman was entrusted with assembling the top aviation engineers in the industry to join him in the hunt for the Luftwaffe's secret aeronautical research—before the Soviets got to it. Among the first people von Karman contacted was Boeing's chief aerodynamicist, George Schairer. At the time, Schairer was in charge of the design for a new bomber, the XB-47.

Military intelligence experts were unsure where the Third Reich's secret aeronautical research facility was located. It turned out to be deep in the countryside of the municipality of Volkenrode, east of Hanover and north of the Harz Mountains. The facility was camouflaged much like Boeing's

Previous spread: The B-47 Stratojet, shown making a rocket-assisted takeoff, was the first U.S. multi-engine swept-wing jet bomber.

Right: Viewers admire a cutaway model of the 377 Stratocruiser. Boeing had high hopes for the elegant passenger plane, but it would be eclipsed by the Douglas DC-6.

wartime plant in Seattle. Hitler had directed that it be destroyed, but with the war nearly over, the research center's superintendent was taking his time. When the Operation LUSTY team arrived, he greeted them warmly and invited them inside. What they discovered would change the course of aviation history and elevate Boeing to the top position as a manufacturer of commercial airliners.

The group uncovered a cache of priceless aeronautical data indicating that the Luftwaffe was far more technologically advanced than previously believed. This intellectual treasure included research reports describing a jet plane with novel wings that were swept back at a diagonal toward the tail, as opposed to crossing the fuselage in the shape of the letter T.

Germany had already produced the first operational jet fighter, the Messerschmitt Me 262, near the end of the war, which looked like a conventional plane, minus the propellers. The new swept-wing jet was a startling departure. The treasure trove of data also included assessments of the unique jet's performance in a German wind tunnel, which indicated it could fly at nearly the speed of sound. The team was awed by the findings.

Even better, they were given the opportunity to interview the facility's director, Adolf Busemann, who had worked with von Karman before the war and was considered the Luftwaffe's top aerodynamicist. Busemann elaborated on the research findings and reminded the group that he had given a paper on swept-wing development at a conference in 1935, which several team members

Douglas returned to its pre-war dominance in passenger aircraft with the DC-6 (left).

Boeing's new high-speed wind tunnel (right), prompted by test pilot Eddie Allen

and finally built in 1944, would prove crucial to the company's development of jet airplanes. The B-47 jet bomber was the first aircraft design tested in the wind tunnel.

had actually attended and recalled. Back then they did not see the promise in the research. Now they had a different reaction: Busemann had all but built a near-supersonic jet.

Seizing on the vital importance of the research, George Schairer dashed off a seven-page letter to his Boeing colleagues that included a drawing of the swept-back wings and key mathematical formulae. He tucked the letter into an envelope stamped "Censored" to ensure that it was delivered immediately. "We'd been searching all these years for ways to make our airplanes go faster, and here was the knowledge," he later said.

Boeing designers and engineers immediately tested the research data in the company's new high-speed wind tunnel in consideration of using the swept-back wings on the new XB-47 bomber. The wind tunnel, competed in 1941 at the behest of test pilot Eddie Allen and at a cost of about $1 million, could reach speeds of Mach .9, just below the speed of sound. "[Schairer] made the very gutsy call to immediately stop all design work on the XB-47 [and] transform it instead into a swept-wing turbojet bomber," said aviation expert Richard P. Hallion.

Schairer's decision *was* risky—Boeing was in competition with other aircraft manufacturers to win a major contract for a next-generation bomber. A revolutionary design might be considered too radical a departure from the propeller-powered planes of the period. But as Bill Boeing had written in 1929, "Let no new improvement in flying

equipment and flying pass us by." Schairer understood the need to seize and adapt to the next technological advancement.

Not only were the jet's swept wings decidedly progressive, but so were the engines. Although the original design for the jet had the engines mounted on the fuselage, the German engineers' research showed that this placement increased the risk of fire. Boeing design team leaders Ed Wells and Bob Jewett decided to mount the engines in pods suspended on struts below the wing. Their wind tunnel tests of the concept proved its merit: the jet's wing performed as if there were no pods attached.

Upon his return to America, Schairer led the effort to develop the XB-47 Stratojet bomber. Among his engineers' concerns was that a swept-wing plane would have less lift compared to traditional straight-wing aircraft, but tests in the wind tunnel indicated that the jet's speed made up for any difference in lift. The wind tunnel revealed other findings that resulted in more than a dozen major design revisions to the original plans and solved complex problems challenging the development of jet airplanes flying at supersonic speeds. The XB-47 was ready for takeoff.

On its maiden flight in December 1947, the jet bomber's performance greatly exceeded that of conventional propeller-powered aircraft. Its narrow swept wing created less drag than a straight wing, permitting the jet to fly at a speed of more than 600 miles per hour, faster than any other aircraft. "When they demonstrated it for the first time to the Air Force, the Air Force sent up a fighter to chase it, and they lost the bomber," said author Clive Irving. "They couldn't find it. The bomber was faster than the fighter. That had never happened before."

Boeing won the contract to build the world's first swept-wing jet bomber, later released to the Air Force as the B-47. In 1948, the government ordered 10 B-47s, which were built at Boeing's Wichita plant. More than 2,000 B-47s ultimately

Right: Upon discovering advanced German jet research, George Schairer immediately wrote a letter to his co-workers detailing the significance of the swept wing.

Far right: The XB-47 Stratojet prototype would use the German research found by Schairer to usher the United States into the jet age.

③

airfoil section normal to the wing and by the sweepback.

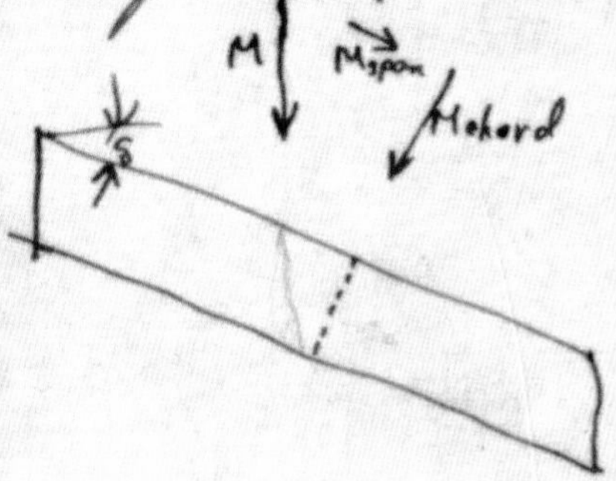

$$M_{chord} = M \cos \delta$$

For instance a 9% wing might have a critical $M = .8$ and an 18% wing $M = .7$. This is a ratio of .875. $\cos^{-1}.875 = 29°$. If the same spars & Merit retained the chord parallel to the wind will be constant and the thickness will increase not by 2:1 but by

①

I go. I have seen Kinnaman & Martin often. There is plenty to eat. Hope things are going well for you. My best to all the gang. They are sure tops in all comparisons.

Sincerely

George

The B-47 (left and right) was the first American plane to feature swept wings and podded engines.

were manufactured, more than a quarter of them by competitors Douglas Aircraft and Lockheed Corporation under a cooperative arrangement similar to what existed during the war. Once again, companies were eager to collaborate and learn from each other's technological expertise and adapt this knowledge for the development of next-generation aircraft.

One initial drawback to the B-47 was its range. The jet needed a large volume of fuel to reach and sustain top speed. Boeing's solution involved another adaptation of the C-97 military freighter. The company developed an aerial tanker version of the C-97, called the KC-97 Stratofreighter, that could refuel other planes in flight using a novel telescoping pipe called a "flying boom," which was akin to a gas station pump in the sky. An operator controlled the boom, positioning it from the tanker into a receptacle on the receiving aircraft. This was a game-changing innovation.

By the mid-1950s, the KC-97 tanker could rendezvous midair with the B-47 Stratojet and quickly transfer large quantities of jet fuel, thus extending the bomber's range. Boeing has been the U.S. military's chief manufacturer of tanker planes ever since.

North American Aviation also benefited from German research in its development of the F-86 Sabre Jet, the country's first swept-wing fighter. The company manufactured more than 6,000 F-86s at its Los Angeles and Columbus, Ohio, divisions. The Sabre was the top-performing jet fighter of its time and was followed by the F-100

The Douglas F4D Skyray (left) was the Navy's first carrier jet capable of supersonic speeds.

North American Aviation's F-100 Super Sabre (right) was the world's first op-

erational fighter to reach supersonic speeds in level flight. The U.S. Air Force used the jets for the Thunderbirds demonstration team from 1956 to 1968.

Super Sabre, which served the U.S. Air Force from 1954 to 1971.

German technical knowledge also would guide the U.S. aircraft industry's development of missiles. The engineer in charge of the devastating German V-2 rocket's design was Wernher von Braun. Despite his former allegiance to the Third Reich, the U.S. government was able to transfer von Braun and a number of his colleagues to America to work in rocket development.

Among them was Rudolph Herman, who in 1946 would help design Boeing's experimental Ground-to-Air Pilotless Aircraft (GAPA), a project initially funded by the U.S. Army Air Forces. The needle-nosed GAPA prototype rocket flew at supersonic speed, launching into the Utah desert sky with a thunderous roar.

U.S. aircraft manufacturers combined the German scientists' knowledge with their own engineering insights to develop a series of extremely innovative next-generation jet aircraft as well as missile and rocket technology. As had been the case from the very beginning, each aviation company's goal was to do better than the others' and its own previous efforts—a process of continuous improvement that is standard operating practice at Boeing today.

Bill Allen led Boeing as the company president from 1945 until 1968. He is shown here boarding a B-47 Stratojet.

Perhaps the person most impressed by the B-47 was Boeing president Bill Allen. Eager to experience the sensation of jet flight, Allen caught a ride on the military jet plane in 1950. As it ascended at 600 miles per hour to an altitude of 35,000 feet, Allen had a transforming experience. The jet traveled so smoothly and quickly, he was convinced that the future of passenger air travel was by jet. "From that moment on, there was no looking back," said aviation writer Guy Norris.

The B-47 altered the trajectory of aircraft manufacturing. For Boeing, the decision to manufacture the jet plane marked a historic transition; it would never again mass-produce a manned propeller plane. And it would never again fall behind chief rival Douglas Aircraft in the airliner market. Plans were now put forth for the 707, the jet plane that would profoundly alter the future of passenger air travel. In the meantime, the evolving Cold War continued to put pressure on American foreign policy objectives, which in turn would generate spectacular advancements in military aircraft, missiles, and rockets.

Data collected from Operation Paperclip were instrumental in the development of experimental Ground-to-Air Pilotless Aircraft (GAPA) missile tests.

Wing technology has continued to evolve since the introduction of the swept wing, as a comparison of the XB-47 Stratojet (left) and a Boeing X-48C subscale unmanned research aircraft (right) shows.

In the postwar world, where atomic bombs were a reality, technological superiority equaled military superiority. Both world superpowers—the United States and the Soviet Union—competed for global influence, inflaming tensions and igniting regional wars. Each invested heavily in a massive array of weaponry that included increasingly advanced jet aircraft, rockets, and missiles.

Because World War II was won in the air, the U.S. military relied heavily on the aviation industry for its next-generation armaments. As Boeing and other manufacturers competed intensely for government contracts, their ingenuity, skill, and continuous improvements would lead to a breathtaking array of advanced aircraft, developed in an extraordinarily short period of time.

Three Cold War developments spurred much of this progress: the Korean War, the nuclear arms race, and the Soviet launch of the Sputnik artificial satellite. The latter contributed to a major expansion in the industry's focus from aviation to aerospace—building aircraft and spacecraft that could travel through both Earth's atmosphere and surrounding space.

The Korean War, which erupted in 1950, was the Cold War's first actual battlefield. During the three-year war, the B-29 Superfortress was the only one of Boeing's planes to see combat. The B-29s of the Far East Asia Forces Bomber Command flew more than 20,000 missions from bases in Japan and Okinawa, dropping 160,000 tons of bombs—more bombs by weight than the United States had dropped in the Pacific during World War II. Later in the war, the Soviet MiG-15 plane proved effective against formations of B-29s, and the plane was relegated to striking targets only in bad weather or at night, when the MiGs seldom flew.

Other U.S. aircraft manufacturers played a larger role in the war effort, with North American Aviation's F-86 Sabre Jet distinguished as the most important jet fighter in Korea. The company's F-82 Twin Mustang was used as a night fighter in the early part of the war, and its F-51D Mustang was flown by a number of United Nations member states to great success. The LT-6G Mosquito, a combat version of the T-6 Texan trainer, was relied on for light ground attacks, and the NAA RB-45C Tornado conducted reconnaissance missions during the Korean War.

Douglas Aircraft Company's planes also were well represented. The A-26 Invader light bomber was used for strike missions, the A-1 Skyraider was the U.S. Navy's primary ground attack airplane, and the F3D Skyknight was deployed by the U.S. Marine Corps as a nighttime fighter.

McDonnell Aircraft improved on its FH-1 Phantom with the larger and faster F2H Banshee single-seat jet fighter, which was assigned by both the Navy and the Marines to ground attack missions. Commemorated in James Michener's novel *The Bridges at Toko-Ri*, the F2H Banshee was the primary U.S. Navy combat aircraft in the Korean War. It carried bombs, rockets, and cannons; a later version could accommodate nuclear bombs.

Another innovative fighter that helped make McDonnell the premier developer of such aircraft was the XF-85 Goblin. The tiny experimental jet was less than 15 feet long, yet its wingspan extended beyond 21 feet fully outstretched (the wings could be folded to five and a half feet in length). In its collapsed state, the Goblin could be tucked into a B-36 bomber and then lowered and

North American Aviation's F-86 Sabre Jet (left) was used extensively during the Korean War. More than 6,000 were ultimately produced.

The F-86D Sabre Jet (far left) was an all-weather interceptor variant of the F-86 with a distinctive nose radome.

Previous spread:
The B-52 Stratofortress has been in active service since 1955.

94

released for protection. Two prototypes were constructed before the government terminated the program in 1949.

The industry also provided aircraft for other purposes such as search and rescue missions to locate and secure downed airmen, transportation of cargo and personnel, and reconnaissance missions. By and large, these planes were just slight improvements over the aircraft of the Second World War. This changed dramatically with the introduction of the B-47 Stratojet, the first swept-wing jet bomber.

The Stratojet series of jet bombers, beginning with the experimental XB-47, introduced a number of technological advancements and established many design parameters for large jet aircraft that exist to this day. Once in the skies, the sleek experimental jet broke speed and distance records, crossing the United States in less than four hours in 1949.

The B-47 quickly became the foundation of the U.S. Air Force's Strategic Air Command, which acquired more than 2,000 of the graceful jets. Entering service during the last weeks of the Korean War in 1953, it did not engage in any combat missions during the conflict, which was winding down. Nevertheless, its very existence was enough to worry the Soviet Union about the nuclear bombing capabilities of the United States. Besides, another jet bomber already was in the drawing stages.

The Air Force had requested that Boeing design a heavy bomber as a successor to the B-47. But military officials were concerned that the sheer size and weight of the aircraft prohibited the use of jet engines. This thinking was understand-

able: the B-47 had 18 small rocket units in the fuselage for jet-assisted takeoff and a drag chute to reduce the landing speed. The Air Force's request led Boeing designers to conclude that a heavy bomber with turboprop engines powering the plane was the best solution. Top company engineers including George Schairer and Ed Wells, who had already drawn up initial plans for a jet-powered heavy bomber, put these designs on the back burner and drummed up ideas better suiting the military's requirements. The Boeing engineers met with representatives from the Air Force at Wright Field Air Force Base near Dayton, Ohio, to discuss the bomber's design. The meeting did not go well. It was immediately apparent that despite the specifics of the bid request, the Air Force in fact did want a *jet* bomber. Colonel Henry "Pete" Warden, Air Force chief of bomber development, reportedly glanced at the drawings the engineers presented and brusquely explained that the Air Force was not in the market for a propeller-driven heavy bomber.

Realizing that the government would reject their design, the Boeing engineers acted quickly. They convened at the Van Cleve Hotel, where they were staying in Dayton, and expanded on Schairer's and Wells's initial drawings for a jet-powered heavy bomber. They reconfigured the aircraft with eight engines and wings swept at 35 degrees with a 185-foot wingspan. In what has become industry legend, Schairer then went to a local hobby shop and bought some balsa wood, glue, paint, and carving tools. Throughout the night in the hotel suite, they fashioned a model of what would become the famous B-52 bomber. "The Air Force bought the concept on the basis of the model that weekend," said author Clive Irving.

From the handmade model to the actual plane, more than three million engineering hours were put into the B-52's development. The two prototypes alone cost a reported $2 million each. The jet was the first swept-wing long-range heavy

bomber in history. At 350,000 pounds, it also was the heaviest bomber ever made and was taller than a four-story office building. The time and expense were well worth it: following the B-52's maiden flight in 1952, Ed Wells reported to the Boeing board of directors that it was "the most successful first flight of any airplane the company has ever built."

The B-52 Stratofortress entered military service in July 1955. Two years later, three B-52Bs completed a 24,325-mile nonstop flight around the world in 45 hours, 19 minutes, at an average speed of 520 miles per hour. During the first decade of its service to the Air Force, the jet was part of the country's strategic defense arsenal, but throughout the Vietnam War it saw extensive service as a conventional bomber. The B-52 also played an important role in the Persian Gulf War of 1991.

Sixty years after its introduction, this vital strategic heavy bomber—updated with new avionics, data-link communications, and other electronic systems—is still in operation. Although it originally was designed as an intercontinental high-altitude nuclear bomber, the jet's operational capabilities were enhanced over the decades to address changing defense needs. The bomber has been reconfigured for low-level and extended-range flights and modified to launch long-range cruise missiles. The B-52 remains the longest-serving bomber in U.S. military history.

The U.S. aerospace industry's long string of remarkable military aircraft continued after the war. In 1956, McDonnell Aircraft introduced the F3H Demon, a subsonic swept-wing U.S. Navy carrier-based jet armed with missiles rather than guns, a first. Another aircraft with a spectral name (James McDonnell had a keen interest in the spirit world) was the F-101 Voodoo tactical fighter, which broke the world speed record in December 1957, flying 1,207 miles per hour. The plane could be used in multiple missions as a long-range

attack fighter, as an interceptor, or for photoreconnaissance, a capability that proved effective during the Cuban Missile Crisis.

McDonnell also used the Phantom name again with the F-4 Phantom II, an all-new two-seat twin-jet fighter. The plane traveled at more than twice the speed of sound and had a range of 1,750 miles, making it the U.S. Navy's fastest, longest-range fighter. From the debut of the prototype in 1959, the Phantom II smashed previous records for speed, altitude, and time-to-climb rate (the time it takes aircraft to reach a certain altitude), and it continued to break its own records in succeeding years. These remarkable attributes were of vital military importance.

The F-4 Phantom II entered service with the Navy in 1960, although both the U.S. Air Force and Marines also would adopt the fighter for their own uses. Intended initially as an interceptor, the in-demand and versatile jet saw service from both aircraft carriers and land bases. "The Phantom II was the linchpin fighter aircraft of the Allies during the Vietnam conflict, highly revered because of its multi-role capability," said former U.S. Air Force Lieutenant General David Deptula. "It could do surface attack, close air support, interdiction, air-to-air combat [and] reconnaissance. It could carry a huge bomb load, greater than a B-17 during World War II, [and] eight air-to-air weapons. It was the right airplane for the right time." McDonnell Aircraft would build more than 5,000 of the big fighters over the next 20 years.

In 1960, Boeing acquired Vertol Aircraft of Philadelphia, adding a new factory location and product line to its portfolio. Vertol had been found-

ed 20 years earlier by engineer and helicopter pioneer Frank Piasecki as the P-V Engineering Forum. The company was well known for its groundbreaking tandem-rotor helicopters such as the HRP-1 Rescuer and H-21 Workhorse. With the acquisition, Boeing became responsible for building and upgrading the CH-47 Chinook and CH-46 Sea Knight tandem-rotor helicopters, which were of vital importance to American military efforts. Chinook heavy-lift transport helicopters logged thousands of hours of combat service during the Vietnam War. In the last days of the war, a lone Chinook reportedly transported 147 refugees to safety in a single trip. The Sea Knight medium assault transport helicopter could take off from water or land and was deployed by the U.S. Marine Corps primarily to carry troops and cargo. By 1968, the Sea Knight had carried half a million troops, hauled countless tons of supplies, and made 8,700 trips carrying the wounded, while Chinooks were responsible for rescuing hundreds of Vietnamese civilians caught in the war zones.

The Soviet Union also spent the postwar years developing highly advanced aerial weapons of war. A new round of Cold War maneuverings was ignited by the Soviet Union's successful launch of the Sputnik 1 satellite into orbit above the earth in 1957. Sputnik was a "major triumph of Soviet intelligence, with immense military significance," the *Seattle Times* ominously stated. Fearing the United States was falling behind technologically, the U.S. government and the aerospace industry strengthened their development of increasingly sophisticated missiles, rockets, and, ultimately, manned spacecraft.

One week after the satellite's launch, the U.S. Air Force announced a competition to design a reusable manned spacecraft capable of orbiting Earth, reentering the atmosphere, and landing safely. The following year, Congress created the National Aeronautics and Space Administration

NASA chose McDonnell to build the Project Mercury spacecraft (left and right). Riding inside the Mercury capsule, Alan Shepard would be the first American in space.

(NASA). The Space Race was on, sparking a dazzling rivalry for supremacy in the heavens. The urgency to win the contest catalyzed U.S. aircraft manufacturers to push the envelope of ingenuity as they competed for—and also collaborated on—a continuing stream of government contracts.

Among the first was a contract with Douglas Aircraft to manufacture a new multistage launch vehicle called Delta. The first stage used a modified Thor intermediate-range ballistic missile. Thor, named for the Norse god of thunder, was originally designed in the mid-1950s to carry thermonuclear missiles that could reach Moscow from bases in England and other allied nations. Although the first Delta launch was unsuccessful, the second, on August 12, 1960, operated smoothly. Delta became one of the world's most active satellite launch vehicles.

McDonnell Aircraft also distinguished itself as a manufacturer of missiles and rockets. Under the direction of founder James McDonnell, known as "Mr. Mac" to his employees, the company built a series of decoy missiles called Quails that were carried and launched by B-52s to confuse enemy radar. Its experimental Alpha Draco missile built on the boost-glide principle of propulsion developed by Wernher von Braun with the V-2 missile during World War II.

As a result of the company's advanced jet fighter, missile, and rocket designs, the U.S. government awarded a historic contract to McDonnell Aircraft: the manufacture of America's first manned spacecraft for NASA's Project Mercury. America's goal was to put an astronaut into orbit around Earth and bring him back safely—before the Soviet Union could do it. The contract called for McDonnell to manufacture a dozen single-person space capsules. NASA initially had selected 110 military test pilots for the project, winnowing the number down, after a series of grueling physical and psychological tests, to seven astronauts, among them Alan Shepard. In January 1961, Shepard was chosen for the first American manned mission into space.

A series of delays postponed the anticipated launch, however. Much to NASA's disappointment, on April 12, 1961, Soviet cosmonaut Yuri Gagarin not only became the first human in space but also the first to orbit Earth. The United States was only one month behind when Shepard became the first American to venture into space on a suborbital flight in May. On February 20, 1962, astronaut John Glenn, aboard the Mercury capsule Friendship 7, became the first American to orbit the planet. The capsule was so small that Glenn famously remarked, "You don't get into it, you put it on." Mercury's success led to McDonnell Aircraft's later development of the capsule for Project Gemini, NASA's second human spaceflight program, preceding Project Apollo.

Although the United States came in second to the Soviet Union in putting both a satellite and a human being in space, President John F. Kennedy pledged in 1961 that the country would be the first to put a human being on the moon, and it would do it before the end of the decade. The goal was so preposterous that many people thought the youthful president was bluffing. The Soviets had put the first dog into space only four years earlier, and now the United States was planning to transport people to and from the moon, 240,000 miles away? "It was such a ludicrous proposal," said Cold War historian Audra J. Wolfe. "But if you were the country that could pull it off, surely you could do anything."

To achieve the goal, Kennedy vowed to outspend the Soviets and build a giant rocket so complex and powerful that it could speed through space at more than 25,000 miles per hour. "To do it first before this decade is out, we must be bold," Kennedy said in a 1962 speech at Rice University.

The president was convinced that NASA, sustained by the American aerospace industry's

inventiveness and manufacturing expertise, would make good on his pledge. The industry had performed beyond expectations during World War II, and aircraft manufacturers had proven their willingness to collaborate effectively on seemingly unachievable efforts of vital import to the country. They also had continually adapted their aircraft to incorporate each other's technological breakthroughs, culminating in progressive advancements at breakneck speed. Certainly the industry could do the same for the space program.

"NASA [realized] we'd never get to the moon if we did it in-house," said aviation expert Howard McCurdy. "Industry would have to do close to 90 percent of the work."

In the industry's corner were von Braun and his fellow German aerospace experts. Sending humans to the moon was something that von Braun had thought about for years and believed entirely possible. A few years later, these unlikely collaborators—top former German scientists, NASA, and the U.S. aerospace industry—would contribute to the most extraordinary feat ever accomplished by human beings.

In the meantime, the nuclear arms race heated up. The pressure intensified to develop missiles and rockets that would serve as effective nuclear deterrents in the defense of North America and its allies. Dutch Kindelberger at North American Aviation had experimented with rockets and missiles since the end of the Second World War. In 1955, he established a separate division in Los Angeles called Rocketdyne to design, develop, and manufacture large, liquid-propellant rocket engines.

The Minuteman intercontinental ballistic missile project (right and far right) used the full range of Boeing's capabilities. The company was in charge of building both the missiles and the silos. At one point almost 40,000 Boeing workers were on the project.

Over the following years, North American would continue to develop innovative electronic technologies to guide, manage, and build remarkable rocket propulsion systems.

One North American Aviation program, the X-15 manned rocket-powered aircraft, was designed to study flight conditions beyond Earth's atmosphere and their effects on the craft and the pilot. Built for the Air Force, the Navy, and NASA, the X-15 was launched from a modified B-52 bomber. The X-15 set an altitude record of 354,200 feet (67 miles) in August 1963 and a speed record of Mach 6.7 in October 1967. Because jets traveling at hypersonic speed—five times the speed of sound or faster—fly into the thermodynamic barrier, the frictional heat on their surfaces is too intense for traditional aircraft metals. Solving this problem by using a special heat-resistant nickel alloy elevated North American as a leader in rocket science. The data provided by the program helped inform the development of subsequent manned space missions.

North American also worked on the government's Navaho project to develop a ground-to-ground supersonic intercontinental cruise missile. The company's experiments bred breakthroughs in computerized guidance systems and other spacecraft features and functions. "The program was just full of new technology in cooling systems, engine systems, propulsion, rockets, and separation of the booster from the vehicle, which [would] become important to the Apollo program in the 1960s," said former NASA program manager Dale Myers.

During this same time, Hughes Aircraft was focusing on making light military helicopters such as the OH-6 Cayuse. Douglas Aircraft pushed boundaries with the Nike Ajax, a long-range anti-aircraft weapon and the world's first operational surface-to-air guided missile. A later version was the Nike Zeus, a three-stage solid-fuel rocket guided by a computerized control system.

At Boeing, although the United States had canceled the GAPA rocket program at the end of the Korean War, remnants of the project spurred other notable developments. GAPA's computer system BEMAC (Boeing Electro-Mechanical Computer) was integral in the development of the Bomarc missile, the world's first long-range anti-aircraft missile and the first missile that Boeing mass-produced. Engineers from Boeing ("Bo") and the University of Michigan Aeronautical Research Center ("marc") initially had designed the pilotless supersonic missile in 1949.

A Bomarc with a range of more than 400 miles launched into the skies for the first time on September 10, 1952. The test flight was a success: the missile shot straight up off the launch pad and through the clouds, leaving a sunlit vapor trail in its wake. Boeing ultimately would build 700 Bomarc missiles between 1957 and 1964. Armed with either a conventional or a nuclear warhead, the missiles were placed in remote areas in 420 individual launch shelters that Boeing also manufactured. They were kept combat ready.

Among Boeing's military projects, none was more important than the long-range, three-stage Minuteman LGM-30 intercontinental ballistic missile (ICBM). In 1958, Boeing was chosen to design and develop the Minuteman, which was capable of carrying multiple warheads. As with the Bomarc contract, the company was also contracted to build hidden underground launch facilities around the country. The deal was a major one. "Virtually all the nation's aircraft and missile firms bid for the coveted assignment," the *Seattle Times* reported the day news of the contract

broke. Boeing president Bill Allen told the paper that while the award was "exceptionally good news" for the company, the Minuteman was "one of the greatest challenges . . . we ever have faced."

He added, "We intend to measure up to it."

Boeing did. Powered by a rubbery mass of solid fuel, the Minuteman LGM-30 entered the Strategic Air Command's arsenal in 1962. Four years later, more than 1,000 Minuteman missiles were operational, buried in underground silos at six sites. As Allen acknowledged, the project was one of Boeing's largest, longest running, and most complex military contracts. The company relied on 35,000 suppliers and more than 18,000 subcontractors for equipment, parts, and services. North American Aviation, for instance, supplied the guidance and control systems. As it had demonstrated during World War II, Boeing could be relied upon to effectively manage its industry peers.

When the Minuteman was delivered to the government on time and under budget, Boeing was extolled as the aircraft industry's most adroit manager of contractors, suppliers, and complex systems.

These many technological fulfillments, while deemed necessary to the country's defense, nonetheless created fears that the United States and the Soviet Union were inexorably marching toward apocalypse. The silver lining was that this research and development would be vital to non-military aerospace projects in the years ahead—applying the industry's success with adaptive architecture to peaceful objectives.

A McDonnell FH-1 Phantom lifts off in the first jet-propelled carrier takeoff.

The F2H-2 Banshee was used for ground attacks by both the U.S. Navy and Marines.

The F-101 Voodoo could serve as a fighter or interceptor; later it was used for photo reconnaissance.

The 707 and the Jet Age

In the postwar period, Boeing and its aerospace competitors had become substantial enterprises engaging in multiple markets: military aircraft, rockets, and missiles; commercial airliners; and space-bound vehicles and satellites. The different ventures provided diversification that moderated the industry's volatile cycles but did not come close to eliminating them. Aerospace would continue to be a risky enterprise in the unpredictable global economic and geopolitical environment.

A case in point is the development of America's first jet-powered passenger airplane—the Boeing 707. The 707 evolved from the B-47 and the swept-wing aircraft research discovered by George Schairer. But there was no guarantee that the American public would be willing to travel on a jet-powered plane and thus no certainty that airlines would abandon their propeller planes and line up to purchase the expensive new jet aircraft. Another challenge was that very few commercial airports in the United States could accommodate jet aircraft, which required longer runways.

"Airlines were wary," said author Geoffrey Thomas. "Jets were gas guzzlers and they were unreliable [and] not yet proven."

Fueling these worries was a widely publicized series of accidents involving British de Havilland 106 Comet commercial jetliners, the first passenger jets. Although the Comet traveled without incident during its first year, problems ensued. Three of the jets exploded or broke apart during flight. The disasters were later attributed to metal fatigue due to the effects of pressurization on stress points at the corners of the Comet's square windows—a problem that American manufacturers, who had more experience with pressurized aircraft, had previously resolved.

Despite hesitation on the part of airlines and the public, Boeing President Bill Allen was convinced jet travel was the future. His decision for the company to invest in manufacturing jet passenger planes, even in the aftermath of the de Havilland failures, required the nerves of a high-stakes poker player. No wonder *Time* magazine called the 707 a "gamble in the sky."

Allen did indeed gamble big. More than 5,000 Boeing designers, engineers, and draftsmen would be tasked over a period of several years with developing the Dash 80 jet prototype. The Dash 80 name derives from the fact that it was the 80th variation that Boeing's designers drafted in their unrelenting efforts to develop a passenger jet airliner. The airplane was eventually named the 707, the first in the famed 7-7 series of Boeing commercial jetliners.

Ultimately, Boeing would sink roughly $16 million into the creation of the Dash 80, an amount equaling approximately one-quarter of the company's net worth. At the time, Boeing was so closely associated with making bombers that critics argued the company had no business being involved in, much less financing, the commercial airliner business. "While Boeing had thrived as a military manufacturer, its performance in the commercial market bordered on the anemic," the *Seattle Times* reported.

The newspaper had a point. In 1950, the company's share of the passenger market was less than 1 percent. Now Allen was betting its future on not just a new airplane but a brand new type

Previous spread: The 707 ushered in an era of passenger jet flight—and Boeing dominance in commercial aviation.

Right: On May 14, 1954, Boeing workers in Renton, Washington, celebrate the rollout of the Dash 80, prototype for the 707.

of airplane. And an extremely expensive one at that—each 707 would be priced at a whopping $4 million at a time when the jet's primary competitor, the propeller-driven Douglas DC-7, cost a comparatively paltry $1.85 million.

Allen was taking a calculated risk, however. He knew the jet's much greater size and speed would enable it to do double the duty of the propeller-powered DC-7. The 707 carried between 140 and 189 passengers and was also smoother riding and easier to maintain than the DC-7. Its appearance was nothing short of dazzling. When the Dash 80 rolled out for its preflight tests in July 1954, reporters and photographers elbowed each other for the best viewing spots. The sleek brown-and-yellow-painted jet was described as having wings that were sharply swept back like a modified jet fighter. When its four jet engines fired up, commentators called the sound a low wail rising to a roar.

"The 707 was one of the most extraordinary airplanes not just in the history of Boeing, but in the history of American commercial aviation," said aerospace historian Tom D. Crouch.

To promote the aircraft, Allen asked company test pilot Tex Johnson to fly the 707 at Seattle's annual Seafair summer celebration at Lake Washington. To Allen's surprise, Johnson executed a slow but perfect barrel roll in the big jet. Spectators were in awe at the stunt.

"He told nobody that he would do a barrel roll, completely turning the plane upside down and back up again," said author Clive Irving. "You don't do this with an airliner, [but] apparently he'd done it at other times in the test program."

Two months after its rollout, the Dash 80 makes its maiden flight. Commercial aviation would never be the same.

Seemingly dazed by the pilot's feat, Allen is said to have popped a heart pill. The next day he called the test pilot into his office. As Irving recounts the tale, Allen "had blown all his gaskets. He was mad. 'Did you realize what you were doing?' And Tex says, 'Yeah, I didn't do anything the plane couldn't do. . . . It was never in an unsafe condition.'"

Needless to say, Johnson's barrel roll earned its fair share of publicity. The public may have felt comfort at the huge jet's remarkable maneuverability, but most airline executives still worried. Not all, however: Juan Trippe of Pan American Airways saw the same promise in passenger-jet travel that Bill Allen did.

As airline industry competition intensified, Trippe was eager to invest in innovative aircraft that would distinguish Pan Am. Passenger jets fit the bill perfectly, and Pan Am became the launch customer for the 707, with an initial order for 20 jets in October 1955.

Trippe asked Allen to keep the contract a secret until the jet's introduction. He wanted to take advantage of the publicity that would undoubtedly arise. In fact, he did not announce the purchase until the 707s were ready for delivery, and then he proclaimed it in characteristic style: at a cocktail party at his apartment overlooking Manhattan's East River on October 15, 1955. The executive committee members of the International Air Transportation Association were present and were reveling in their companies' recent purchases of new turboprop planes when Trippe announced that Pan Am was going all jet. One could hear a pin drop as the executives absorbed the statement's significance—their brand-new turboprops had just become obsolete. The Jet Age had arrived without them knowing it.

The first scheduled transatlantic 707 flight by Pan Am took off from New York to Paris on October 26, 1958, and Trippe went all out to treat the event like the premiere of a major Hollywood film. The 112 passengers walked to the boarding stairs on a red carpet flanked by red-velvet cords draped from brass stanchions. The jet, known as *Clipper America*, was illuminated by floodlights at Idlewild Airport (John F. Kennedy International Airport today). Before takeoff, First Lady Mamie Eisenhower christened the Boeing 707, and Trippe gave a speech saluting the plane as a triumph of the American spirit.

Both Allen and Trippe took substantial risks on the 707. And they hit the jackpot. The plane was soon the wonder of the skies. "The 707 obliterated time and distance as it soared across the country, capable of streaking from Seattle to New York in less than five hours," the *Seattle Times* wrote.

At cruising altitudes of 30,000 to 40,000 feet, the jet could cross the Atlantic Ocean in hours rather than the days a ship required. In an October 1960 article, *New Scientist* compared the passenger capacity of the 707 to the *Queen Mary*. "In the twelve days needed to send the ship across the Atlantic and back with a potential load of 3,000 people each way, the Boeing, crossing twice in a day, could carry 2,040 … [The *Queen Mary*] is unlikely to be able to compete in profitability with the air route."

Neither could the DC-7 or any other propeller-powered plane. Allen had proved the wisdom of his gamble, and Boeing eventually would sell more than 1,000 707s. The Dash 80 prototype was also adapted into the KC-135 tanker, a jet that could refuel other military jets in flight.

Allen scored a win with both planes, again proving the advantages of adaptive architecture. "He endured the swarming gnats who think small,"

The new 707 provided a quicker, smoother, more comfortable flight. Promotional materials featured families (right and far right) to assure passengers of the safety of the jet planes.

Fortune magazine wrote in a 2003 cover story naming Bill Allen one of the 10 greatest CEOs of the 20th century. "Allen thought bigger."

Competitors soon followed Boeing's dashing entry into the Jet Age. Douglas Aircraft's first long-range jet, the four-engine DC-8, entered service with Delta Air Lines in September 1959. Advertisements gushed that the jet's "lounges are almost like clubs!" and that the "world's most relaxing jetliner" had wide aisles, broad seats, and "individual lighting built right into your seat." But this time Boeing had the winning hand, racking up more sales with the 707 than Douglas with the DC-8. Never again would Douglas best Boeing in the sale of commercial airliners.

By the end of the decade, all the major U.S. carriers and prominent foreign airlines had ordered the new jet planes produced by Boeing and its competitors. They engaged in high-stakes competition for passengers, boosting the fortunes of Madison Avenue advertising agencies. Both the airlines and the aircraft manufacturers continued to assertively portray jet air travel as safe. Boeing, for instance, advertised the 707 as America's "most tested airliner ever to take to the skies." Other ads reassured travelers that flights would be "restful, serenely quiet." Another pledged passengers would be "so completely free from vibration [they'd] be able to stand a half-dollar on edge."

The 707 was also marketed as a luxurious alternative to transatlantic cruise lines. "In this superb ship, you will cruise indigo blue skies six miles above the earth—with such serene smoothness you'll seem poised motionless in space, yet be traveling at an incredible 600 miles per hour," a Boeing advertisement claimed. Other ads touted the jet's speed, pointing out, "The flower you bought when you left will be fresh when you arrive."

Travel on the new passenger jets was also promoted as being available to everyone, not just to affluent flyers. In the 1950s, the United States

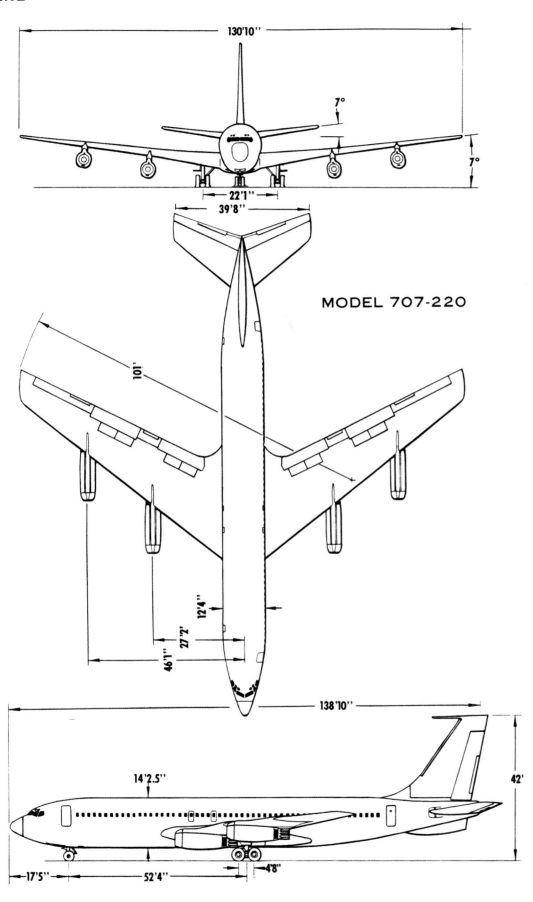

MODEL 707-220

was in the middle of an economic boom. The public's disposable income rose appreciably, giving many Americans the financial means to vacation abroad.

This democratization of air travel was supported by basic economics. By transporting more passengers in larger planes traveling greater distances, airlines could charge reduced fares. For the first time, pretty much anyone could take to the skies. Increasingly, people did just that: the volume of passengers carried vaulted from 16.7 million people in 1948 to 35.5 million in 1954. Passenger travel had more than doubled in just six years.

These are remembered as the glamour days of jet travel, when boarding a plane was an event akin to boarding a cruise ship—an occasion people dressed up for. Prior to takeoff, the pilots walked up the aisles, giving children enameled metal pins with flight wings on them. Passengers in all classes received printed menus from which they could order a variety of free entrées and cocktails. Elegantly attired flight attendants served food and beverages to passengers, who dined on seatback tray tables, a novelty.

Once they were in the air, the biggest surprise for many first-time jet passengers was the noise— or lack thereof. Flight attendants no longer had to hand out earplugs. The only surprising sound passengers heard was the whine of the landing gear being elevated and lowered. In the days of piston-engine aircraft, the engines had drowned out this sound.

Flying in a jet plane became the thing to do. Celebrities who traversed the world by air were described as being members of the Jet Set. Even the president of the United States traveled on a 707. Beginning in President Dwight D. Eisenhower's term, air traffic control crews used the call sign "Air Force One" to designate the plane used to transport government officials. The name stuck after the government ordered two Boeing 707-

320B airframes to be adapted specifically for use by President John F. Kennedy. To this day, Boeing jets are the official transport of the U.S. president.

Ultimately, the 707 became the standard for all passenger jets and the forerunner of more than 14,000 Boeing commercial jets built since its debut.

"They kind of got it right the first time around at Boeing with the 707," said author Sam Howe Verhovek. "If you think about it, we're not really flying any faster today or more comfortably than when the Boeing 707 first took off."

The company had a winner in the 707 and was amenable to adapting the airliner to carrier wishes. When Qantas, Australia's largest airline and a longtime purchaser of Douglas planes, needed a jet with greater range than the conventional 707-120, Boeing's engineers shortened the fuselage by 10 feet, giving the jet greater fuel efficiency. Qantas purchased 13 of the unique 707-138s.

As in the past, industry competition spurred many aircraft advancements that, in turn, led to other technological achievements. When the 707's success spurred Douglas and other manufacturers to switch to jet-driven planes, their respective expertise and ingenuity would advance Boeing's own research and development. The marketplace also played a role in these iterative enhancements. For example, when Pan Am indicated that it would buy 25 DC-8s from Douglas and only 10 707s from Boeing because the DC-8 had capabilities the 707 lacked, Boeing's engineers redesigned the 707 with a wider body, a more powerful engine, and bigger

A schematic of the 707-220 (left) shows the plane's dimensions.

In 1962, two 707-320B jets were adapted for use by President John F. Kennedy, earning the designation "Air Force One" when the president is on board (right). Since then, Boeing 7-7 series airplanes have continued to be the official aircraft of the U.S. president.

wings. The improvements increased fuel capacity from 15,000 gallons to more than 23,000 gallons and gave the jet a range of more than 4,000 miles when in a 141-seat configuration. Excluding the six DC-8s that had already been shipped, Pan Am eventually switched its entire order to Boeing. The new plane was known as the 707-300 Intercontinental.

On May 28, 1959, the Intercontinental made a record nonstop flight of 5,830 miles from New York to Rome. A later version, the 707-320B Intercontinental, could fly nonstop over a distance of 6,000 miles, thanks to another innovation: turbofan engines. This revolutionary jet engine received additional thrust from a new turbine-driven fan. The turbofan remains the engine of choice for virtually every commercial and military jet aircraft today.

As commercial aircraft manufacturers gradually produced larger and wider-body jet planes with added features and functions, the economics of air travel continued to improve. An astonishing parade of innovations came forward. Boeing's three-engine 727, for instance, was the first jet to undergo rigorous fatigue testing, the first to have completely powered flight controls, the first to use triple-slotted wing flaps, and the first to have an auxiliary power unit. The jet, which had three engines mounted below the tail, also could be convertible. Although it typically accommodated 131 passengers, sections of seats could easily be removed to permit greater cargo capacity. The aircraft, designed to service smaller airports with shorter runways on domestic routes, made its maiden flight in November 1966. Its range was

A sleeper success, the adaptable 737 continues to evolve and post strong sales more than four decades after its introduction.

3,110 miles, and its top speed was 632 miles per hour.

Boeing's next jet in the 700 series was the narrow-body 737, which was intended to compete in the short-haul category. In its initial 100-seat configuration, it offered six-abreast seating, a selling point with airlines because it carried more passengers per load than the competitors. Like the 727, the 737 operated well at smaller airports and even remote, unimproved landing fields—the latter prompting orders by airlines in Africa, Central and South America, Asia, and Australia. The 737 would eventually become a legend in the aerospace industry and the best-selling airliner of all time; the 8,000th 737 rolled out of the factory in April 2014. Today Boeing estimates that, on average, more than 2,000 737s are in the air at any given time, with one of the jets taking off or landing somewhere in the world every two seconds.

By 1962, more than 30 million passengers on 27 airlines had traveled the world on a Boeing plane, and the company was besting all rivals in the commercial jet transport business. The following year, Boeing was in the black on the program-development costs for the early 7-7 series, including the $16 million invested in the Dash 80 prototype.

With the 707, Boeing entered the Jet Age and defined the new financial dynamics of the aerospace industry. Constant innovation, risk taking, and mastery of increasing complexity were the levers that aircraft manufacturers had to pull to stay alive in the increasingly competitive business. Subsequent projects took much longer to reach fruition yet still required a dizzying speed of production. Manufacturers needed vastly more resources, and to provide a return on their investments, they had to disrupt the status quo and be game-changers. This new way of doing business required a combination of visionary leadership, courage in the face of uncertainty, and a die-hard resolve to complete the most difficult projects imaginable.

Boeing's entire 7-7 series of jetliners, lined up numerically from the 707 on the right to the 777 at the left, was on display during the new 787 Dreamliner's premiere.

To the Moon and Beyond

23

The Cold War between the United States and the Soviet Union was as much a battle of ideas as it was a series of regional conflicts. Each of the superpowers jockeyed to be the technological leader of the world. Throughout the 1960s, the United States lagged behind the USSR, which had put the first satellite and first human being in space. President John F. Kennedy had tasked NASA with the goal of landing astronauts on the moon by the end of the decade in part because he was aware of the importance of global scientific leadership. This was one "first" the United States did not want to lose.

The bulk of this extraordinary effort would fall on the shoulders of the American aerospace industry. Much as they did during World War II—when Boeing, McDonnell Aircraft, North American Aviation, and Douglas Aircraft augmented each other's skill and expertise and collaborated to win the war in the skies—aerospace companies allied to win the race to the moon.

"They wanted to participate in what they saw as a national enterprise, something that would be worthy of national glory," said science historian Asif Siddiqi. "They were proud to do it. And their cooperation was very crucial to the success of Apollo."

Project Apollo was NASA's third (after the Mercury and Gemini projects) and most ambitious spaceflight program, conceived with an audacious purpose: ferrying astronauts to and from the moon. Nowhere was the industry's shared legacy more profound than in Project Apollo's nine manned and unmanned expeditions to the moon between 1969 and 1972. Virtually all of Project Apollo's spacecraft and launch vehicles, including

the Saturn V rocket, Apollo command and service modules, and Lunar Roving Vehicle, were designed, developed, and built by Boeing and the aerospace manufacturers that would later become part of it.

Each manufacturer possessed a wide array of scientific, technological, and engineering skill sets. Their combined efforts represented a mobilization of American industry that had not been seen since the end of the war—the arsenal of democracy was again collaborating toward a shared national purpose, tackling the most complex project in history at the time.

"There were 400,000 Americans who worked on [Project Apollo]," said former NASA astronaut Frank Borman. "They were all dedicated and they all wanted to win. That was the key. We win. They lose."

Winning meant the program would need to carefully design, develop, test, and take a series of challenging technological steps leading to the eventual landing of astronauts on the moon. To assure safe landing sites for the manned Apollo command module, for instance, Boeing built crewless Lunar Orbiters to circle and photograph the moon's surface. The five orbiters had to operate precisely because photos could only be taken under the proper light and temperature conditions.

The first picture of Earth rising above the moon's cratered surface in 1966, taken by Lunar Orbiter 1, was hailed by many as one of the greatest photographs of the 20th century. People were awed seeing the planet from such a perspective.

Tellingly, the photograph was snapped at roughly the halfway point of Boeing's 100-year history. In just 50 years, the company had gone

Previous spread: An astronaut uses the Boeing-built Lunar Roving Vehicle to explore the terrain of the moon.

Right: A mock-up of the Boeing-built Lunar Orbiter is displayed above a model of the moon's surface.

SATURN V APOLLO FLIGHT CONFIGURATION

A. APOLLO SPACECRAFT

B. APOLLO LAUNCH ESCAPE SYSTEM (LES) *
   B—1 PITCH MOTOR
   B—2 TOWER JETTISON MOTOR
   B—3 LAUNCH ESCAPE MOTOR

C. COMMAND MODULE (CM) *
   C—1 CREW COMPARTMENT AND CONSOLES

D. SERVICE MODULE (SM) *
   D—1 REACTION CONTROL SYSTEM (RCS)
   D—2 ENVIRONMENTAL CONTROL SYSTEM,
      COMMUNICATION AND INSTRUMENTATION,
      ELECTRICAL POWER FUEL CELL BATTERIES,
      PROPELLANT TANKS
   D—3 PROPULSION SYSTEM ENGINE

E. I.U./APOLLO INTERSTAGE ADAPTER

F. LUNAR EXCURSION MODULE (LEM) *

G. LEM LUNAR LAUNCH STAGE *

H. LEM LUNAR LANDING STAGE *

I. THREE STAGE SATURN V LAUNCH VEHICLE

J. LAUNCH VEHICLE INSTRUMENT UNIT (I.U.)

K. S-IVB THIRD STAGE
   K—1 FORWARD SKIRT
   K—2 FORWARD BULKHEAD
   K—3 HELIUM SPHERES
   K—4 MAINTENANCE PLATFORM
   K—5 HYDROGEN TANK
   K—6 COMMON BULKHEAD
   K—7 LOX TANK
   K—8 AFT SKIRT
   K—9 ULLAGE ROCKETS
   K—10 AFT BULKHEAD
   K—11 J-2 ENGINE

L. S-II / S-IVB INTERSTAGE SHROUD
   L—1 RETRO ROCKET

M. S-II SECOND STAGE
   M—1 MAINTENANCE PLATFORM
   M—2 FORWARD BULKHEAD
   M—3 FORWARD SKIRT
   M—4 FORWARD SUPPORT RING (GSE)
   M—5 INSTRUMENT CONTAINER *
   M—6 CONTINUOUS TANK PROBE
   M—7 HYDROGEN DIFFUSER
   M—8 HYDROGEN TANK PRESSURE RECEIVER (2)
   M—9 HYDROGEN TANK
   M—10 GAS DISTRIBUTOR
   M—11 LOX VENT LINE
   M—12 LOX RECIRCULATION LINES
   M—13 PROPELLANT LOADING
   M—14 LOX TANK
   M—15 COMMON BULKHEAD
   M—16 HYDROGEN FILL AND DRAIN
   M—17 RING SLOSH BAFFLE
   M—18 AFT BULKHEAD
   M—19 HYDROGEN LINE
   M—20 LOX FILL AND DRAIN LINE
   M—21 J-2 ENGINE (5)

N. S-IC/S-II INTERSTAGE ADAPTER
   N—1 S-II STAGE AFT SUPPORT RING
   N—2 INTERSTAGE ACCESS DOOR
   N—3 ULLAGE ROCKET (8)

O. S-IC FIRST STAGE BOOSTER
   O—1 INSTRUMENT CONTAINERS
   O—2 FORWARD BULKHEAD, LOX TANK
   O—3 FORWARD SKIRT
   O—4 LOX TANK VENT LINE
   O—5 GOX DISTRIBUTOR
   O—6 GOX LINE
   O—7 RING SLOSH BAFFLES
   O—8 LOX TANK
   O—9 HELIUM BOTTLE (4) *
   O—10 CRUCIFORM BAFFLES
   O—11 ANTI-VORTEX DEVICE
   O—12 AFT BULKHEAD, LOX TANK
   O—13 LOX FILL AND DRAIN LINES
   O—14 INTERTANK
   O—15 INTERTANK ACCESS
   O—16 FUEL VENT LINE
   O—17 FORWARD BULKHEAD, FUEL TANK
   O—18 FUEL PRESSURE LINE
   O—19 HELIUM DISTRIBUTOR
   O—20 FUEL TANK
   O—21 SUCTION LINE TUNNEL (5)
   O—22 LOX SUCTION LINE (5)
   O—23 ENGINE FAIRING (4)
   O—24 FUEL DUCTS (10)
   O—25 THRUST STRUCTURE
   O—26 RETRO-ROCKET
   O—27 FIN (4)
   O—28 THRUST VECTORING SYSTEM
   O—29 UMBILICAL PLATE
   O—30 F-1 ENGINE (5)

* ROTATED FOR CLARITY

from making an open-cockpit biplane out of wood and cloth to creating an unmanned metal craft that could circle the moon and take pictures of Earth.

As planning for the Apollo missions progressed, NASA and the aerospace industry relied heavily on Wernher von Braun and the hundreds of other German engineers and technicians brought to the United States after the end of the war.

Von Braun was put in charge of developing the Saturn V rocket, the powerful multistage liquid-fueled rocket that would serve as the launch vehicle for the Apollo lunar craft. Saturn V involved three propulsion stages. Boeing was in charge of building stage one, North American Aviation was responsible for stage two, and Douglas Aircraft for stage three. North American's Rocketdyne division made all the engines. The rocket was composed of more than three million parts and 700,000 components, and much of this technology was original.

"Each one of those parts has to meet thousands of individual specifications and requirements to make sure it does its job, that one part," said Boeing chief technology officer John Tracy of the challenge. "And then all those parts have to come together . . . and work together without fail."

All three stages of the rocket were critical and required unparalleled collaboration among the three aerospace manufacturers. For liftoff, more than 203,400 gallons of kerosene fuel and 318,000 gallons of liquid oxygen were needed. Once ignited, the first stage's five F-1 rocket engines produced more than 7.5 million pounds

The Saturn moon rocket was an example of collaboration among aerospace companies. Boeing was in charge of the rocket's first stage (far left); North American, the second stage; and McDonnell Douglas, the third stage. North American's Rocketdyne built the engines for all three stages.

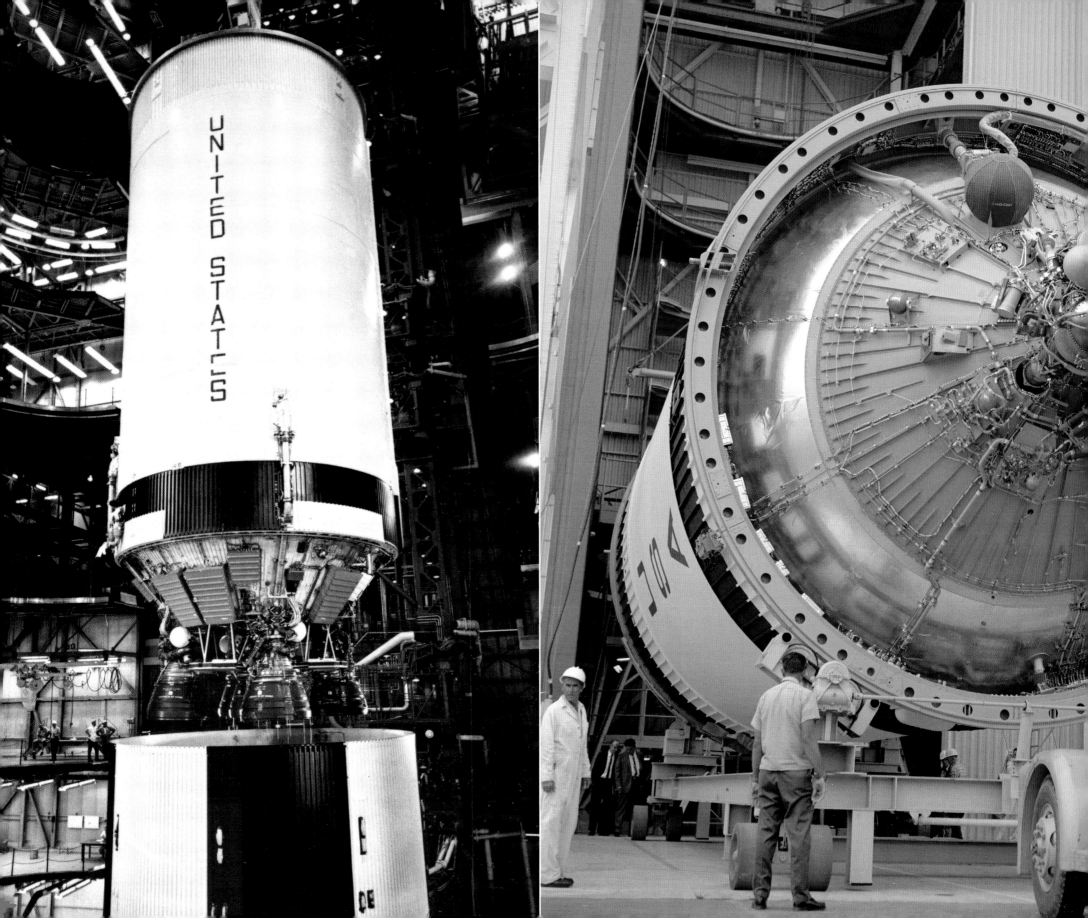

The Saturn V multistage liquid-fueled rocket was the launch vehicle for the Apollo missions. The Saturn V second stage is shown at far left; third stage at left; and Rocketdyne J-2 engines at right.

of thrust, creating more power than 85 Hoover Dams. At an altitude of 42 miles, the second stage ignited as the first stage disengaged from the launch vehicle. Then, at nine minutes and nine seconds into the launch, the third stage's engines fired and the second stage was discarded.

To provide the heavy lift needed to launch the lunar craft to the moon, Saturn V had to be not only complex but gargantuan. Fully fueled, the rocket weighed 6.2 million pounds and was taller than a 36-story building.

Boeing became the technical integrator and coordinator of the Apollo project following a devastating fire in the command module during preparations for the first crewed Apollo flight in 1967. Three astronauts—Gus Grissom, Roger Chafee, and Ed White—perished in the disaster, compelling NASA to reach out to Boeing for help. Boeing President Bill Allen responded, "We'll help the nation in any way that NASA wants."

NASA and Boeing entered into a historic Technical Integration and Evaluation (TIE) contract to support Apollo by strengthening the program's management to avoid another safety setback in the quest to reach the moon by decade's end. Allen assigned more than 2,000 Boeing managers to assist NASA, while dozens of others worked on the overall systems integration.

Management of the integration effort was entrusted to George Stoner, vice president and general manager of the Boeing Space Division. Stoner was responsible for ensuring that the millions of pieces of hardware making up the spacecraft's myriad components were in perfect working order. He was also in charge of the space project's schedule.

Because reliable, secure communications were crucial, Boeing worked with a number of

Apollo 11 lifts off the launch pad on July 16, 1969.

major U.S. companies including Xerox, AT&T, and Western Union to establish the Blue Network, a dedicated system connecting key managers at NASA facilities with Boeing personnel.

The first Saturn V was launched, unmanned, as Apollo 4 in 1967. The first successful manned mission was Apollo 7 in October 1968; it used the Saturn 1B rocket. The first manned mission involving the Saturn V launch vehicle was Apollo 8, which orbited, but did not land on, the moon. Piloted by Frank Borman, Apollo 8 reached the moon on December 24, 1968. "A machine of that size, of that scope, working perfectly—unbelievable," Borman said.

The importance of the historic flight cannot be overstated. Borman and fellow crewmates Jim Lovell and Bill Anders were the first human beings to see Earth as a bright-blue planet, the first to reach the moon, and the first to orbit the moon—10 times over the course of 20 hours. They had traveled farther than anyone had gone before, and without a lunar module to take them back if something went wrong. As they circled the moon that Christmas Eve, they read verses from the Book of Genesis as millions listened and watched from their television sets at home. They snapped another iconic photograph of the planet and broadcast it to the world, this one in full color—Mother Earth as a vividly alive world spinning in the vastness of space.

The launch of Apollo 11 in 1969 finally achieved President Kennedy's vision. Astronaut Neil Armstrong became the first human being to walk on the surface of the moon. The Apollo 11 command module that transported Armstrong and fellow astronauts Edwin "Buzz" Aldrin and Michael Collins to Earth's only natural orbiting satellite was designed and built by North American Rockwell, which along with Boeing was the industry's primary architect of the Apollo program.

For U.S. aerospace manufacturers, their ability to work together effectively and successfully on

the most daunting project in history was meaningful beyond compare. "They all knew they were involved in an immensely satisfying effort, and they really worked together in ways that probably never could have happened in any other program," said former NASA deputy administrator Dale Myers, who had been in charge of the Apollo Command/Service Module at North American at the time of Apollo 11. But it was not the first time they had pulled together for an important project, nor would it be the last.

Although Boeing's contribution to the Apollo program was not a moneymaker and its costs would contribute to the company's financial stress during the 1970s, the work nonetheless provided a wealth of newfound knowledge that would contribute both to its future space endeavors and to more traditional enterprises. Chief among these lessons was how to make aerospace vehicles of greater reliability.

When NASA began preparing for the Space Shuttle program in the 1970s, North American Rockwell was selected as the prime contractor. Unlike previous once-and-done spacecraft, NASA wanted the shuttle to be a reusable transport system—a freight truck in the sky hauling modules and components into space to build the planned International Space Station, deploy satellites, and someday serve as a launch pad for trips to Mars. To meet NASA's objectives, North American's Rocketdyne division developed the first reusable liquid fuel engines for the vehicle.

Although creation of the Space Shuttle orbiter fell largely to North American Rockwell, Boeing's

The North American Rockwell-built Apollo Command/Service Module is shown in orbit above the moon (left).

It took the cooperative efforts of many cutting-edge companies to put humans on the moon (right).

Artists' renderings depict the Dyna-Soar space vehicle (left) and an early Space Shuttle concept (right). Dyna-Soar was canceled before a prototype was made, but it shared similarities with the Space Shuttle as it ultimately evolved.

Dyna-Soar, an earlier 1960s project to develop a crewed, reusable space vehicle, played an instrumental role. Later designated the X-20, the futuristic space vehicle featured sharply swept wings, a graphite-and-zirconia composite nose cap, and three retractable struts for landing. Eleven manned flights of the X-20 were scheduled, but the government canceled the program in 1963 because it had no applicable military mission.

North American Rockwell's first orbiter for NASA was named *Enterprise* after a write-in campaign by fans of the *Star Trek* television series, which featured a spaceship of that name. Although NASA's *Enterprise* was an approach-and-landing test vehicle that had no capability to fly into space, it helped guide the development of the next shuttle orbiter, the *Columbia*, the first space shuttle to fly into actual orbit. The *Columbia*'s many triumphs include the first launch of a satellite from a space shuttle and the first flight of the European-built scientific workshop, Spacelab. It made 27 successful round trips. Near the end of its 28th mission in 2003, the *Columbia* disintegrated upon reentry, resulting in the deaths of all seven crew members aboard. It was the second such disaster after the loss of the shuttle *Challenger* in 1986.

Over the course of 135 missions through the end of the Space Shuttle program in 2011, the fleet of five shuttles deployed an astonishing array of satellites, stargazing telescopes, and astrophysical instruments. The many components of the International Space Station relied on this space transportation system, as did the deployment of the Hubble Space Telescope. When either needed repair, parts and technicians flew on board a shuttle to service them. The shuttle also had the capability to recover malfunctioning satellites in orbit and return them to Earth for repair and possible relaunch.

The people of North American Rockwell (later Rockwell International) and Boeing played a huge

part in making the program possible, but the effort was not their sole focus. Simultaneously, these companies and others in the aerospace industry were putting their respective skills toward manufacturing and launching satellites. Leading the effort this time was Hughes Aircraft.

Following the launch of Sputnik in 1957, Hughes engineers and scientists were intrigued by the communications possibilities that could be afforded by satellites circling the planet. Sputnik was a basic satellite that merely beeped out its location. Harold A. Rosen, an engineer at Hughes, envisioned an array of advanced satellites connecting with television, telephone, and other broadcast signals on Earth and beaming them back across the world. This system would be far more effective and cost-efficient than the physical wires and undersea cables providing global communications at the time.

Rosen drew up his concept for an unmanned geostationary satellite that would circle the globe at exactly the same rotational speed as the planet. In effect, the robotic satellite would be stationary above a fixed point on the planet and would synchronously rotate with Earth. From a distance of 22,300 miles, the satellite could receive and transmit communications signals from approximately one-third of the planet's surface. Radio and television antennas on the ground would be directed precisely toward the satellite. Three satellites could connect the entire globe. It was a mind-blowing idea.

"Most of the people I talked to thought it was pretty wild," said Rosen. "And it was."

Hughes Aircraft was initially reluctant to invest in the concept, as it did not fit the company's traditional military and commercial manufacturing focus. Other problems loomed: while many engineers were impressed by the science behind Rosen's idea, the practicality of transporting a heavy satellite by rocket to its geostationary resting place that far from Earth was questionable, as

was the mechanism by which the satellite would stay in place.

These misgivings soon gave way, in large part because of the promise of this vast communications network and the ingenuity of Rosen and the engineers at Hughes. For instance, they developed lightweight satellites that were made of small-scale components and used thin antennae. The small, cylindrical craft, which measured just 28 inches in diameter by 15.35 inches high, could be put into orbit by the elementary rockets then available. They also developed the idea of spinning the satellite like a gyroscope to help it remain fixed in place. Two tiny jets, one powered by nitrogen and the other by hydrogen peroxide, would keep the satellite from drifting off course.

On behalf of NASA's Syncom (synchronous communication satellite) program, the first experimental satellite, Syncom 1, was launched in 1961, but the satellite's electronics system failed. Two years later, Syncom 2 was successfully placed in orbit. A few weeks later, President John F. Kennedy phoned the prime minister of Nigeria from the White House. It was the first live two-way conversation between heads of state involving a satellite. Syncom 3 ushered in the first international television broadcast, transmitting signals from the 1964 Olympic Games in Tokyo to the United States.

"I remember to this day the young man running down with the torch and lighting the flame," said Rosen. "It just felt great."

In succeeding years, Hughes Aircraft would manufacture satellites for countries including Malaysia, for commercial enterprises such as XM Satellite Radio, and for military applications such

A conceptual illustration portrays the operation of Syncom, the first geosynchronous communications satellite.

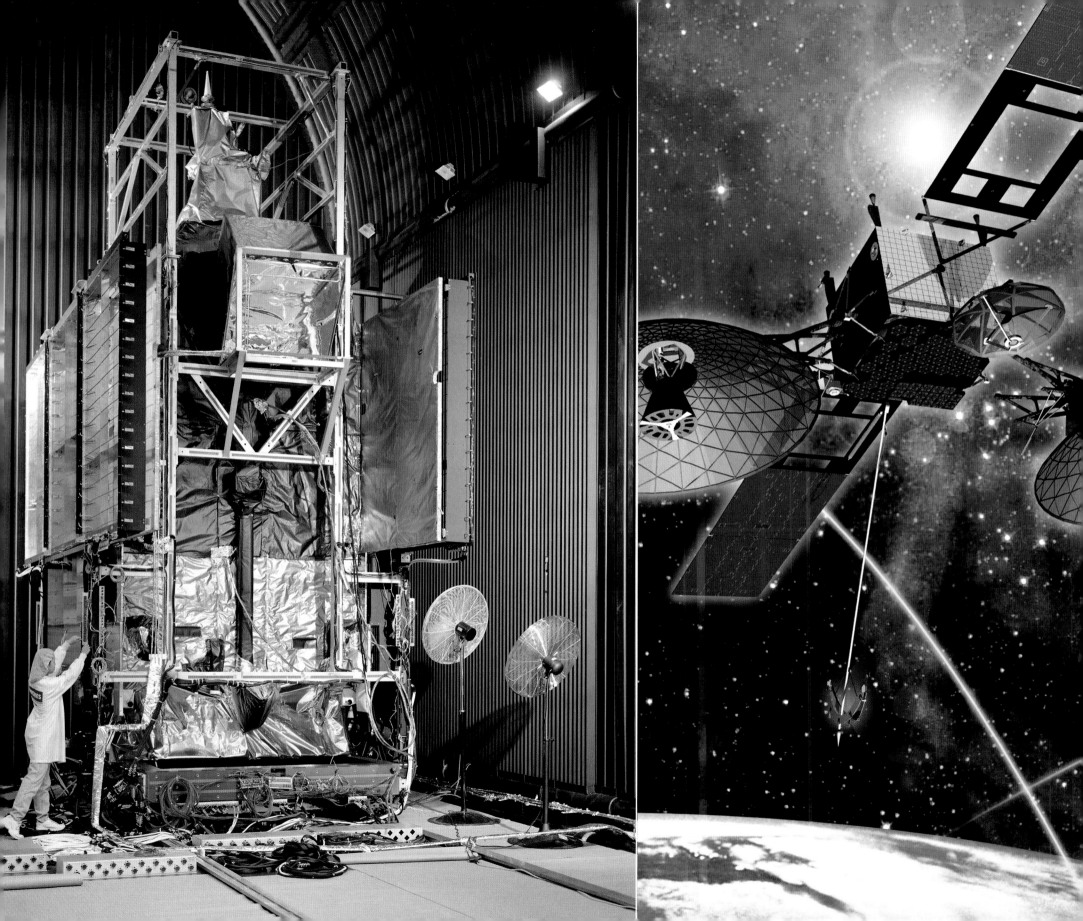

as the Milstar F-6 satellites operated by the U.S. Air Force to provide secure and jam-resistant worldwide communications. The company opened vistas of an interconnected world that was previously the province of science fiction. A half century later, people across the planet would send texts, photos, email, and videos to each other on mobile devices—messages instantaneously beamed back and forth by a constellation of satellites.

Once Hughes had proven the practicality of satellites, the rest of the aerospace industry entered the market. In October 1972, Boeing launched its 72-1 Scientific Satellite, which circled Earth a total of 26,375 times during its first five years of sun-synchronous circular orbit, ultimately logging more than 637 million miles. More important to future satellite development, Boeing applied its technological ingenuity to developing additional satellite applications. Company engineers studied the possibilities of solar-powered satellites affixed with enough silicon solar cells to generate electric energy from sunlight and beam it down to power U.S. cities. The idea was feasible—an early prototype indicated a very large satellite could produce 10,000 megawatts of usable power, enough electricity for one million homes—but not economically viable.

Numerous satellites were launched in subsequent years, among them the 601 satellite, one of the best-selling models in the world today. Introduced by Hughes Space and Communications in 1987, the 601 addressed industry needs for high-power, multiple-payload satellites used for such applications as direct television broadcasting. A more powerful version, the 601HP, made its debut in 1995, featuring up to 60 transponders. Building on the 601HP's success, Hughes unveiled the 702HP satellite in 1999. It carried more than 100 high-power transponders to deliver the broadest range of communications frequencies to commercial customers.

Other manufacturers made their contributions as well. In February 1989, a McDonnell Douglas Delta II rocket launched the first fully operational Global Positioning System (GPS II) satellite into orbit. The prime contractor for the satellite was Rockwell International. Today, a network of GPS satellites provides accurate location information to millions of military and civilian users all over the world on devices as small as a watch or cell phone.

Just as the original aviation industry pushed physical boundaries to allow humans to leave the ground, the new aerospace industry put humans and human technology beyond our atmosphere. The giants of aviation had once again defied the odds.

In 1929, Bill Boeing said, "Science and hard work can lick what appear to be insurmountable difficulties." His statement proved true—even for such fantastic notions as space-traveling human beings and instantaneous global communication.

A Boeing technician prepares a 702 communications satellite for service (left).

An artist's rendering (right) depicts the 601 Tracking Data and Relay Satellite in operation.

The Queen of the Skies

Juan Trippe and Bill Allen had become good friends by the mid-1960s. The leaders of Pan Am and Boeing had conducted plenty of business together over the years, closing deals adding up to hundreds of millions of dollars. The two had even wagered a $25,000 bet on the delivery of Pan Am's 707 jets. If the planes were delivered ahead of schedule, Allen won $25,000. Behind schedule, and Trippe got the money. It was Boeing's president who cashed the check.

There were few subjects the men enjoyed talking about more than the aerospace business and the future of air travel. So it was not unusual that when these titans of industry were on a fishing trip, Trippe brought up Pan Am's interest in flying bigger jet planes able to transport a larger volume of passengers. He could grasp the economics of such jets: lower aggregate costs per available seat mile due to greater fuel efficiency and higher passenger density, among other factors. This would encourage lower passenger fares, making air travel more affordable to the masses.

Allen was all ears. "Trippe told Bill, 'If you build the airplane, I'll buy it,'" said Boeing chief engineer Joe Sutter. "And Bill told him, 'Well, if you buy it, I'll build it.' And they shook hands."

The casualness of their agreement did not take into account the huge challenge that lay ahead: building the largest passenger jet in the history of the industry. At the time, the biggest planes carried no more than 250 people. Trippe was looking for a jet that would transport 450 passengers, nearly double that capacity. "They were as audacious as anybody who had ever lived," said author

Robert Daley. "Both would go bankrupt if they failed. . . . They were in over their heads."

Allen tasked Sutter with leading the engineering effort to build the giant jet. Sutter quickly realized that the aerodynamics of an aircraft of the size Allen and Trippe wanted required a radically new type of plane. Unlike the 707, 727, and 737, the 747—the model number given the immense jet—would not be another iteration. It would be the first of its kind. "It wasn't a minor step at all, it was a big step," said Sutter.

Early meetings between Boeing engineers and Pan Am executives on the 747's design did not go exactly as planned. In Trippe's mind, a much larger aircraft meant a double-decker jet along the lines of London's popular two-story buses. This concept was problematic, however. As Sutter explained to the Pan Am head at a meeting in Boston in 1965, two decks would create complications with evacuating passengers from the upper deck in an emergency. There also would be difficulties loading and unloading the galley, and very little room would be left for freight. Sutter lobbied for a different configuration: a wider fuselage instead of an elevated one.

To demonstrate how wide the plane's cabin would be, Sutter and his fellow engineers brought along a 20-foot length of rope. They stretched it from one end of the hotel conference room to the other and then informed the Pan Am executives that they were sitting inside the wide-body jet. The engineers unveiled two mock-ups, one of Trippe's requested double-decker and the other of the wide-body. "As soon as Juan Trippe saw the wide single deck, he changed his mind instantly," Sutter said.

The design called for a twin-aisle jet with two and a half times the capacity of the Boeing 707. The aircraft would be as long as a city block and as tall as a six-story building. Its wingspan of nearly 196 feet would be more than half the length of a football field, or 76 feet longer than the

Previous spread: The 747 earned the title "Queen of the Skies."

Right: Longtime friends Boeing president Bill Allen (on the left) and Pan Am CEO Juan Trippe (at right) sealed the deal for the 747 with a handshake while on a fishing trip.

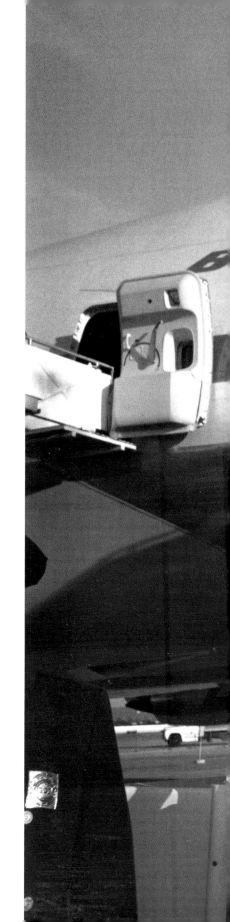

distance traveled during the Wright brothers' first flight. The jet's maximum takeoff weight—735,000 pounds—would require an entirely new 16-wheel landing system to support its huge mass upon landing.

In April 1966, Trippe ordered 25 747s for roughly $525 million. To build a jet of such substantial proportions, Boeing required a more spacious manufacturing plant. In June 1966, the company purchased more than 750 acres of land adjacent to Paine Field in Everett, Washington, roughly 30 miles north of Seattle. More than 250 subcontractors and 2,800 construction workers cleared the dense forest, ultimately moving more earth than had been moved to build the Panama Canal and the Grand Coulee Dam—combined.

The plant was completed in less than a year. At 200 million cubic feet, it was the largest building in the world by volume and, with later additions, remains so today. Building the factory was pure misery. Two months of nonstop rain, followed by mudslides and snowstorms, challenged the workers. When the plant was finished, it was so voluminous that it actually generated its own weather. Clouds formed inside the building, requiring the installation of a state-of-the-art air circulation system.

Five months before the facility opened in May 1967, Boeing employees were already at work in Everett receiving supplies and construction materials, which were delivered via a five-mile railroad spur with the second steepest grade in the country. An army of more than 50,000 Boeing designers, engineers, scientists, mechanics, and administrators joined them in the new building. Boeing executive Malcolm Stamper, who led the project to build the 747, called them "the Incredibles." The name stuck.

While the building and railroad spur construction was under way, the jet's designers were at the drawing boards refining their plans. The initial design drew from a military cargo plane proto-type created for a government-sponsored competition that Boeing lost to another manufacturer, Lockheed. The designers ultimately provided more than 75,000 drawings to Sutter and other key engineers to produce the final design. The jet had a main cabin with 10-abreast seating and a smaller upper deck, above the cockpit, reached by a spiral staircase. The latter was a consequence of the configuration of the cockpit, which was placed on a shortened upper deck so the jet's nose could open as an optional loading door for oversize cargo. This accommodation gave the 747 fuselage its distinctive hump.

Needless to say, the small upper deck was of great appeal to Trippe. Although it was not the double-decker jet he originally had in mind, it nonetheless offered room for more passengers.

The aircraft's large size required an exceptional engine. Eighty-seven tests of different engine configurations were undertaken, resulting in the failure of 60 engines. Boeing engineers finally found what they sought: the industry's first high-bypass turbofan engine, manufactured by Pratt & Whitney. The unique engine delivered double the power of earlier turbofan engines yet consumed less than a third of the fuel.

The 747 also was the first aircraft designed with a new methodology called fault tree analysis, a deductive investigation in which the potential failure of a single part was microscopically analyzed to determine its impact on other systems. In testing the plane, Sutter estimated that his team conducted at least 14,000 hours of wind tunnel experiments using exact-scale nine-foot-long models of the jet, and they exhausted more than 10 million engineering labor hours in the endeavor.

Plans for each new iteration in the plane's design landed on chief engineer Sutter's desk with

Inside the Boeing plant in Everett, Washington, the first 747 takes shape (left).

60 WASHING MACHINES

460 SEWING MACHINES

BOEING 747 FREIGHTER CAPACITY

Not just a passenger plane, the 747 could carry a stunning amount of cargo; its design allowed for cargo to be loaded through the hinged nose of the plane (left).

The distinctive hump at the front of the 747 fuselage houses the cockpit and a short upper deck (right).

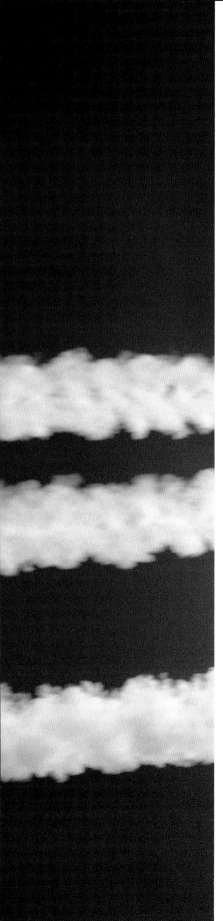

a thud. Trippe visited Everett many times to check on the jet's progress and always left requesting a few additional design changes. The Incredibles took it in stride. "We were a team," Sutter said. "We had a job to do. And people were here to get that job done."

The engineers worked seven days a week, 10 hours a day to do it. "Instead of coming into an empty engineering office at six or seven in the morning, I'd find hundreds of engineers already here," Sutter said. "At the end of the day, I didn't walk out of an empty office."

The endless design changes and scheduling complexities took their toll, creating huge budget overruns. Resources were stretched thin not just by the work on the 747 program, but also by Project Apollo and another major contract with the government to build a supersonic transport (SST) jet. Sutter continually requested that Allen provide more engineers for the 747, but none were available. Capital quickly evaporated, and the company had to reach out several times to its banking partners for additional funding. Anxiety levels soared. "It was literally a race against time to keep the company solvent and deliver the plane," said author Clive Irving.

This race involved more than just Boeing personnel. Stamper had organized a vast subcontractor network to build different parts of the jets, involving thousands of suppliers in "one of the largest industrial efforts in history," the *Seattle Times* reported.

Despite these many obstacles, the Incredibles ultimately pulled off a "heroic feat of engineering," Irving said. They made the deadline with weeks to spare.

The new jet, which made its first flight in September 1968, became known as both the Queen of the Skies and the Jumbo Jet. Several configurations of the 747 were developed: an all-passenger jet, an all-cargo jet, a half-freight and half-passenger jet called a Combi, and a convertible model with the proportions of the seating versus the cargo holds directed by buyers. The convertible model was transformed from a passenger plane into a freighter by removing the seats and adding rollers to the floor to move cargo on pallets. Once Boeing filled Pan Am's order, 26 other airlines also placed orders, totaling $3 billion, for 158 747s in all. As the *Seattle Times* reported, "They stepped up quickly . . . envisaging improved passenger appeal and airline economics with the giant super jet."

Chief among these economics was the volume of passengers that could be flown in the plane—up to 490 people, although many buyers planned on a smaller 360-seat configuration, which was still twice the normal seating of a 707 or DC-8. To entice travelers, the same newspaper article noted, "The emphasis in 747 service will be on 'living room comfort.'"

The 747 would prove to be Bill Allen's crowning achievement. "He had the courage to go ahead with a project that would revolutionize air travel," said Sutter. The jet's radical size, shape, and technological ingenuity became an icon of the modern age. No other manufacturer made an airplane like it. The 747 also deepened impressions regarding what became recognized as one of Boeing's core competencies: integrating large-scale systems involving thousands of people and parts. The 747 and the Apollo program were colossal achievements for a company that a little more than half a century earlier was making biplanes in a boathouse.

Yet at Boeing some considered the Queen of the Skies to be a less important endeavor than the company's work on the proposed SST. Flying

The 747's range and high passenger capacity changed the way the world traveled, opening up affordable, long-distance flights to more people.

The 747 was known not only for its technological achievements, but also for its glamour. With a lounge, cocktail service, and sometimes even a piano, it held the promise of an elegant, relaxing travel experience (left and right).

faster than the speed of sound, the supersonic jets were expected to attract numerous airline buyers interested in promoting shorter flight times to passengers. "Everyone figured the 747 would be an interim airplane until the supersonic jets took off," said Sutter.

The U.S. government had launched a competition in 1966 for a partially funded contract to build an American supersonic transport vehicle. Boeing had been studying the design and development of SSTs since 1952, and in 1958 it had established a permanent research committee to enrich these evaluations. On New Year's Eve in 1966, the company received a belated Christmas gift: news that it had won the competition.

The mockup of the Boeing 2707-300, the model name for the SST, was 318 feet long and fronted by a double-jointed, needle-shaped nose that would drop during takeoff and landing for improved pilot visibility. It was large enough to seat as many as 300 passengers and could cruise at speeds in the range of Mach 2.7. These features made Boeing's proposed aircraft much larger and significantly faster than competing designs like the Concorde, which was jointly developed by Aerospatiale and the British Aircraft Corporation. Once Boeing won the competition to design the aircraft, 26 airlines stepped up to order 122 of the jets. Along with the Apollo program and the 747, the SST associated Boeing in the public mind with unsurpassed technological ingenuity. The company's future seemed boundless.

Similarly, McDonnell Aircraft's F-4 Phantom II jet had established McDonnell as a company capable of technological leaps. But the mid-1960s

were a difficult period financially for the company, which suffered from cyclical downturns in military procurement. Douglas Aircraft also fared poorly, its narrow-body DC-8 jet at a disadvantage as the world's airlines increasingly turned to wide-body aircraft.

Unlike Boeing, which had pursued a balanced postwar market diversification strategy, McDonnell and Douglas had tended to specialize in either military or commercial aircraft, not both. The two companies sounded each other out about a possible merger. Given McDonnell's prowess making military aircraft and Douglas's success with commercial airliners, they appeared to be a good fit. In 1967, they reached the decision to merge and combine the respective strengths of the two companies. The new McDonnell Douglas Corporation was run by Mr. Mac himself: 68-year-old James Smith McDonnell.

Three years later, McDonnell Douglas celebrated the maiden flight of its first wide-body jet, the DC-10, a three-engine plane capable of carrying a maximum of 380 passengers. Two years after the 747 was rolled out, Boeing's wide-body had some real competition. Lockheed also entered the market with a wide-body trijet, the L-1011 TriStar.

American Airlines ordered 25 DC-10s; that order was followed by 30 orders from United Airlines. More than 440 DC-10s were delivered before the last one rolled off the assembly line in 1988.

North American Aviation also entered into a merger in 1967, in its case with Rockwell-Standard Corporation, which was primarily a supplier of automotive parts. After a series of subsequent mergers, the company ultimately became Rockwell International in 1973. During the previous decade, North American had introduced the XB-70 Valkyrie, a stiletto-shaped supersonic bomber designed to fly at three times the speed of sound. But the advent of intercontinental ballistic missiles and other developments rendered the project unnecessary

A CH-46A Sea Knight transfers cargo between two ships. Boeing transport helicopters such as the CH-46 Sea Knight and CH-47 Chinook carry out military and humanitarian missions around the world. The CH-47 serves the defense forces of 18 countries, including the United States.

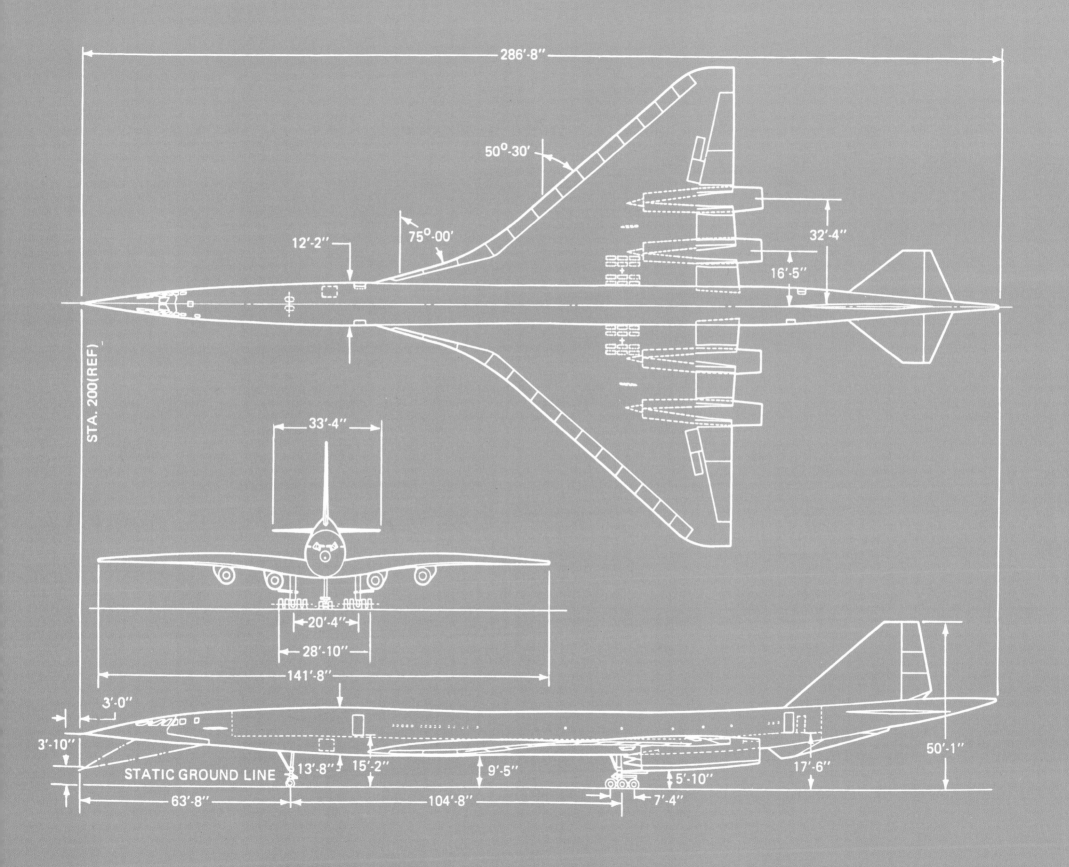

After more than a decade of planning and competition, the contract for the supersonic transport (SST), shown in a schematic diagram (left) and artist's rendering (right), was awarded to Boeing in 1966. The program was canceled in 1971, before the first prototype was complete.

before it went into production, and only two proto-types were made.

As the 1970s commenced, the economic boom that had ignited in the postwar years fizzled for the entire aerospace industry. Boeing and other manufacturers were buffeted by a "perfect storm" of rising fuel costs, falling passenger revenue, and jetliner overcapacity. Carriers had simply bought too many planes, and many now sat idle. The industry had not experienced such difficult times since the Great Depression.

At Boeing, the impact was felt quickly. Fortunately, Thornton Wilson—or T. Wilson, as he preferred to be called—had succeeded Bill Allen as president of the company in 1968. (Allen became chairman of the board, a position he would occupy for the next four years until his retirement.) Although he took command at the pinnacle of Boeing's success with the 747, Wilson turned out to be equally adept at steering the company through a storm. He was as straightforward, unassuming, and unpretentious as his predecessor, although his language was a bit saltier (more than once, Wilson's remarks resulted in letters to the company scolding his use of swear words). An aeronautical engineer by training, he had hired on at Boeing in 1943, right after college, and later headed the company's Minuteman missile program.

Wilson soon confronted substantial challenges. NASA temporarily halted progress on the Apollo space program. With the slowdown in airline orders, the financial outlook was bleak: Boeing's earnings fell from $83 million in 1968 to approx-

The F-4 Phantom II fighter (left and right) first took to the skies in 1958 and was in service with the U.S. military for the next four decades. It served in both the Vietnam War and Operation Desert Storm.

imately $10 million the following year. The pressure took a toll on Wilson, who suffered a near-fatal heart attack in January 1970. He considered retiring but decided to press on, despite the difficult decisions before him.

Over the next 22 months, Boeing's workforce was slashed from 107,962 employees to 61,826. The layoffs had particular impact in Seattle, where the workforce fell from about 80,400 to approximately 37,200. The severe downsizing had an impact on the city's morale; the mood was captured unnervingly by a billboard two real estate agents erected displaying the words "Will the last person leaving Seattle turn out the lights?"

The media were critical of the company's perilous financial state. "Heady with euphoria of the early jet age in the 1960s, Boeing grew fat and sloppy," *Time* magazine chided. "Seattle's entire economy went into a slump."

The final straw was the government's decision in 1971 to no longer fund Boeing's development of the SST, the project once deemed more important to Boeing's future than the wide-body 747. Although airlines remained interested in the concept of supersonic travel, it received wide negative press. Environmental groups complained about the noise produced by the jet's sonic boom and the impact the high amount of fuel it burned had on the ozone layer of the atmosphere. Rising alarm spurred public protests, prompting Congress to withdraw funding in 1971, before the Boeing prototype was ever finished.

Although the SST had consumed huge amounts of company resources and capital, Boeing had no recourse but to cancel the program. The SST became known as "the airplane that almost ate Seattle." Today, what is left of the mock-up of the needle-nosed jet is in storage at the Museum of Flight's restoration center in Everett. But the company never abandoned its research into supersonic flight.

Soaring inflation, interest rates, and unemploy-

ment gripped the United States, constraining economic growth. Business in each segment of aerospace—military, space, and commercial—fell fast. Struggling to pay for the long war in Southeast Asia and new social welfare programs, the U.S. government sharply curtailed military orders. The same factors slowed the sprinting Space Race to a walk. The passenger jet business was equally stagnant: instead of ordering new aircraft, major airlines held on to the planes they had to serve declining passenger loads.

Boeing's formerly robust sales of 7-series jets were anemic. The company even endured an 18-month period, beginning in 1970, in which it did not receive a single airline order. "It was a matter of survival," Wilson later told reporters.

To reduce corporate expenses, Wilson further pared the labor force to about 32,500 in 1971. Local media dubbed the severe downsizing the Great Boeing Bust. A familiar joke of the period was that a Boeing optimist brought lunch to work, while a pessimist left the car running in the parking lot. Even with substantial layoffs, analysts predicted the company was headed toward bankruptcy. Boeing survived from airplane delivery to airplane delivery.

The leaner company held on the best it could. Military programs such as Minuteman missiles and orders for Airborne Warning and Control System (AWACS) aircraft generated needed income. AWACS jets were modified 707s, with the military designation E-3, that carried surveillance radar and other systems to detect and track both airborne and maritime targets more than 200 miles away. The radar was housed in a 30-foot-diameter rotodome, which resembled a giant Frisbee mounted on two struts over the fuselage.

Boeing's various diversifications also buttressed the bottom line. Boeing Vertol in Philadelphia, which usually manufactured military helicopters, received a contract to build light rail

vehicles in Boston and San Francisco and rapid transit cars in Chicago. Boeing Engineering and Construction built large wind turbines for the Columbia River Gorge in Washington State, and Boeing Marine Systems manufactured commercial and military hydrofoils. The company's 13 different computing organizations, each supporting different operations, were combined in 1970 as Boeing Computer Services, an independent subsidiary that would develop an extraordinary range of communications and information technologies in the years ahead.

Other ventures included managing housing projects for the U.S. Department of Housing and Urban Development, converting seawater to freshwater for a Virgin Islands resort, and building radio transmission voice scramblers for police departments. Although these contracts and others provided much-needed income, they were a far cry from the large orders of military jets and passenger airliners from previous years.

The company's biggest asset during this bleak period turned out to be Wilson, who remained optimistic and confident the company would weather the recession's impact. Throughout the crisis, Wilson adhered to the company's practices of innovation and long-term strategic planning. He put an enormous amount of capital—more than 7.6 percent of sales—into the research and development of future aviation technologies and products. Among these were satellites, which were just beginning to become a major market in the early 1970s. "When we get moving, watch out," the ever-upbeat Wilson said.

During the 1960s, Boeing had demonstrated again that it could envision the impossible and then create it. The 747 program had used all of the company's trademark skills: a knack for tackling intensely complex projects, the ability to meet near-impossible expectations, and a passion for creating the best aerospace vehicles. For the time being, however, Boeing's primary enterprises were in a holding pattern.

McDonnell Douglas's first wide-body jetliner, the three-engine DC-10, has accumulated more than 25 million hours of revenue travel since its inaugural flight on August 29, 1970.

The Business of Success

Boeing took advantage of the economic downturn of the 1970s to reevaluate its business prospects and risks, reappraise its skill sets and core competencies, and determine how best to capture opportunities when the inevitable turnaround came.

This strategic introspection guided a virtual reinvention of the company in the 1980s. Transformative geopolitical and technological shifts were under way at the time, including the winding down of the Cold War; the development of revolutionary technologies such as the personal computer and computer-aided design and manufacturing; and the emergence of the Internet. This fundamental reshaping of the world was both a promise and a challenge for Boeing's future business growth.

By 1977, the company had begun to show signs of a rebound from the previous years' woeful financial conditions. That year, customers ordered 228 airliners at a combined value of $4.1 billion—nearly double the value of orders received the prior year. More than half were for the 727, the world's best-selling jetliner at the time. The 747 also continued to sell well, with 300 jumbo jets in the skies in 1977 and another 100 orders for additional planes placed by the decade's end.

Many economic signs indicated that the industry's boom-bust cycle was shifting again: inflation began to taper off, the U.S. gross domestic product saw several consecutive years of growth, and employment and median household income increased. Buoyed by the improving conditions, Boeing CEO T. Wilson announced the development of not one new Boeing airliner but two—the 757 and 767. With its earnings up by 75 percent in 1979 and an order backlog worth $11 billion, Boeing could finance the $3 billion development

cost of the new planes out of its own earnings. "Wilson doesn't expect to have to borrow a dime," *Financial World* magazine reported in 1979.

The two jets would help the company compete more effectively in the shorter-range jet market, which was growing fast. Passenger capacity of the aircraft ranged from 200 to 300 people. Developed simultaneously, the 757 and 767 shared many features—they were nicknamed the "medium twins"—making production, maintenance, and flying easier and more efficient.

Pilot training, for instance, was simplified by the jets' common flight deck, and pilots could fly both airplanes with the same type rating, even though the narrow-body 757 had a single aisle and the wide-body 767 had twin aisles. The jets also were the first to replace conventional electro-mechanical gauges with a two-crew "glass cockpit" featuring cathode-ray tube displays for most of the primary instruments. For pilots, the changes reduced the workload involved in managing an airplane's systems.

Both jets were also versatile; the 767, for example, was later converted into a tanker. And they were fuel efficient and produced less noise—business and regulatory necessities in the post-energy-crisis era.

The jets' new features "reaffirm the company's reputation for innovative technology and superior metal bending," *Fortune* magazine reported in 1982. "The cathode-ray display screens [in the cockpit] would do a video arcade proud." The article quoted former astronaut Frank Borman, then CEO of Eastern Air Lines, stating, "The cockpit far exceeds anything I saw during the Gemini and Apollo programs."

Both jets sold well. United Airlines ordered 30 767s, American Airlines and Delta Air Lines each ordered 50 transcontinental versions of the 767, and British Airways and Eastern Airlines each ordered 40 757s. More than 1,000 757s have been delivered to more than 50 customers, while more

Previous spread: The 777 was the first commercial jet to be 100-percent digitally designed.

Right: The 757 and 767 jetliners share many features, including a computerized "glass" cockpit.

than 1,100 767s have been ordered by some 71 customers worldwide.

At the same time that Boeing was developing the two jets, a new kind of competition was emerging from an unexpected source. European aviation manufacturers had long lagged behind their American counterparts, despite designing and developing many innovative aircraft through the years. The French, German, and British governments now stepped in to discuss the merits of a collaborative pan-European venture. In December 1970, these meetings led to an agreement to establish Airbus Industrie.

The new competitor initially drew little attention from the major U.S. aerospace companies. Other smaller manufacturers had come and gone through the decades without leaving a ripple. "There was probably an element of arrogance in the U.S. aerospace sector when Airbus was created," said aviation consultant Loren Thompson. "The presumption was that this was a political initiative that could not possibly succeed."

Airbus could not easily be dismissed, however. Other European governments added their financial clout to the consortium, while Spain joined its neighbors as a full member and Italy and Belgium signed on as associate members for selected aircraft programs. Slowly but surely, the upstart carved inroads into the market.

In 1972, the consortium's first aircraft, the Airbus A300—a short-to-medium-range wide-body airliner—made its maiden flight. The jet was the first in the industry to be built using just-in-time manufacturing, a mode of production in which parts and materials are made available only as needed, reducing inventory costs and reducing waste. In a then-radical new commercial manufacturing process, complete aircraft sections were built by Airbus partners across Europe and then airlifted to France for final assembly.

Sales were slow at first, but the A300 caught the attention of the U.S. aviation industry when Eastern Air Lines ordered 23 of the twin jets in 1978, citing their fuel efficiency as a draw. Orders from Pan Am and a number of Asian airlines followed. No longer could Airbus be dismissed as just another fleeting competitor.

However, Boeing was flourishing as the economy recovered, with sales just short of $10 billion in 1980. Employment picked up sharply, reaching 109,098 workers the same year. Each month, 25 planes rolled out of production. Once again, Boeing had gone from the brink of bankruptcy to the pinnacle of market success.

Glowing reports replaced the negative publicity that had hounded the company just a few years earlier. In 1981, the Association of Professional Flight Attendants publication *Skyword* featured a cover story titled "Boeing: 'King of the Sky.'" The article noted the remarkable success of its 700 series of "beautiful transports."

They were more than just beautiful. The 747 was the world's largest plane in production, the 727 and 737 were the best-selling twin jets, the 707 had flown more revenue miles than any other airliner, and both the 757 and 767 were racking up their share of orders.

"A stirring recovery is all but in the bag [for Boeing], by far the most profitable of the big aerospace companies," *Financial World* stated in 1981. "[It] is so far ahead of every other maker of commercial aircraft that at times it appears to have no competition."

Military orders also grew in the 1980s. Chief among these for Boeing was the highly competitive $4 billion contract from the U.S. Air Force to develop an air-launched cruise missile (ALCM)

The 767 (left) and 757 (right) were designed with commonality in mind. This meant that pilots, mechanics, and other workers could be easily certified to work on both types of airplanes.

system. *Time* magazine, in an April 7, 1980, cover story on T. Wilson, called the ALCM "a key weapon in the nation's nuclear arsenal . . . to maintain a strategic edge over the Soviet Union." The missile, launched from a B-52 bomber, was known for its pinpoint accuracy over a range of 1,500 miles.

The early part of the decade also boomed for McDonnell Douglas, which continued to build on its strong position as a producer of military aircraft. The company's F-15 Eagle—a twin-engine, all-weather tactical fighter designed to achieve superiority in aerial combat—entered service with the U.S. Air Force in 1974. It remains one of the world's elite air-to-air fighters, capable of launching an anti-satellite (ASAT) missile for strategic military purposes.

On its heels came McDonnell Douglas's F/A-18 Hornet supersonic combat jet, which entered service with the U.S. Marine Corps and Navy in 1983. The Hornet was the first tactical aircraft designed from the outset to accomplish both air-to-air and air-to-ground missions. The versatile jet could even switch mission capabilities in the middle of a mission, if necessary. The Hornet also was the first tactical fighter to use digital fly-by-wire flight controls and the first with carbon-fiber wings. The single-seat F/A-18E and dual-seat F/A-18F Super Hornet jets, introduced in the mid-1990s, were even larger and more versatile than the original Hornet.

Other vital military jets followed. In 1986, McDonnell Douglas unveiled the F-15E Strike Eagle, an all-weather multi-role strike fighter with an unparalleled range and weapons load, which was derived from the F-15. With a highly effective air-to-ground capability and modern avionics

systems, the Strike Eagle could perform air-to-air or air-to-surface missions at all altitudes, day or night, in any weather. The jet is considered the backbone of the U.S. Air Force today.

In 1984, McDonnell Douglas acquired Hughes Helicopters, one year after the first AH-64 Apache attack helicopter rolled out of the Hughes factory in Mesa, Arizona. The tough all-weather Apache, with its formidable weapons array, quickly became indispensable to the U.S. Army. The AH-64D Apache Longbow, which first flew in 1992, added fire-control radar to the combat-proven helicopter's capabilities. Today, the AH-64 Apache is the centerpiece of the U.S. Army's all-weather ground-support capability, carrying a combination of laser-guided precision Hellfire missiles, 70-mm rockets, and a 30-mm automatic cannon. To date, more than 1,800 Apaches have been delivered to customers around the world.

McDonnell Douglas complemented its formidable arsenal of military aircraft with crucial weapons systems, such as the BGM-109 Tomahawk cruise missile and the AGM-84D Harpoon anti-ship missile system, originally developed for the U.S. Navy and now sold all over the world.

While military contracts represented the majority of McDonnell Douglas's business, the company also made inroads on the commercial side in 1980 with the MD-80 airliner, a single-aisle twin jet based on the popular Douglas DC-9. More than 1,100 MD-80s ultimately were produced in six variants, and the jet became the basis for the MD-90 and MD-95 jetliners unveiled in the early 1990s.

In contrast with its rival, Boeing still derived 90 percent of its revenue from passenger airliner orders—a good portion of that from sales of the 737. Versatility, reliability, and a constant modernization program accounted for much of the continuing popularity of the company's smallest jetliner, and the company enhanced its features on a near-annual basis.

The McDonnell Douglas F-15 Eagle was designed as an air superiority fighter—and with a record of more than 100 victories and no losses in air-to-air combat, it has proved to be highly successful in that role. Versatile and rugged, it remains in production more than 40 years after it first entered service.

Boosting the 737's steady sales was approval from the U.S. Federal Aviation Administration for the jet to fly 120-minute extended-range twin-engine operations (ETOPS). ETOPS provided the most direct routing to destinations that previously were off limits to twin-engine aircraft. The aircraft could now fly a greater distance from suitable alternative airports en route. All Boeing jetliner twin jets have earned ETOPS ratings, yielding significant reductions in travel times and fuel consumption, especially on long overwater routes.

Thanks to T. Wilson's leadership, Boeing was well positioned to take advantage of the business upswing. During the 1970s, he had made decisions to severely downsize, earmarked more capital toward research and development, promoted adaptive architecture principles to build on the technological successes of competitors, and prepared for the inevitable economic rebound with a long-term view that considered the types of aircraft that buyers would need and want.

"Wilson's stiff medicine brought Boeing back from the brink," *Financial World* stated in 1981. "Every dime Boeing has spent . . . has helped make production faster and better. There are now more people working for Boeing than there were before Wilson's draconian cuts—109,000 in all."

By the middle of the 1980s, airline traffic across the planet had surged to the highest volume in history. In 1985, Boeing's commercial customers ordered 390 airliners valued at $14.9 billion. The next year brought another $16.3 billion in sales, and the year after that $20.2 billion. In the last year of the decade, Boeing announced that it

The 777 (right) introduced many innovations, including its digital design process and use of new materials such as carbon fiber.

had received orders for 963 commercial aircraft totaling a staggering $47.5 billion.

Frank Shrontz succeeded Wilson as CEO in 1986. Shrontz had worked at Boeing early in his career before leaving to become assistant secretary of the U.S. Air Force. Upon his return to the company, he was named vice president and general manager of the 707/727/737 division and, later, Boeing president.

The company's market lead continued under Shrontz through the 1990s, a decade marked by several breakthrough technological achievements. Among them was the first all-new Boeing airliner in a decade: the 777 long-range wide-body jet, which the company began developing in 1986. The 777 was digitally designed using a three-dimensional computer-aided design/computer-aided manufacturing (CAD/CAM) system. This revolutionary design process permitted more efficient representations of shapes, sizes, and surfaces. Boeing engineers could simply simulate the geometry of an airplane's design, eliminating the costly and time-consuming manufacture of physical mock-ups.

The 777 was designed to be the widest and most spacious passenger jet in its class, able to transport more than 300 passengers more than 10,350 miles. Its ability to travel such long distances was supported by two factors: the jet's engine was the largest-diameter turbofan of any aircraft hitherto manufactured, making it highly fuel efficient; and its design used an improved aluminum alloy known as 7055 in the upper wing skin and stringers (the stiffening members in a wing, fuselage, and tail). The 7055 aluminum alloy weighed less than conventional alloys and offered better compression strength and corrosion and fatigue resistance.

Other unique materials in the 777 included carbon fiber embedded in toughened resins used in the tail and in the cabin floor beams. Ultimately, composite materials such as carbon fiber ac-

counted for 12 percent of the airliner's overall structural weight.

For the first time in history, airlines had the option to use a large, efficient twin-engine jet to fly long-distance routes. Carriers could expand their networks with long routes that were not traveled frequently enough to support a larger aircraft. Adding to the 777's allure was its early ETOPS safety rating for 180 minutes rather than the then-standard 120 minutes. United Airlines placed the first 777 order in 1990, and the jet entered service in 1995. To date, some 60 customers have ordered more than 1,750 777 jetliners.

With the 777, Boeing also broadened its production-sharing agreements with equipment and materials suppliers in other countries. Boeing had partnered with these firms before; in 1974, for instance, it had signed a contract with Mitsubishi in Japan to produce inboard flaps for the 747. But the company's global collaboration efforts grew markedly with the 777. In the 1960s, the amount of 707 content produced outside the United States was around 2 percent by value; by the 1990s, the outside content in a 777 accounted for 30 percent by value.

While Boeing was in the thick of developing the 777, Airbus Industrie quietly toiled in the background, improving its aircraft design and engineering capabilities. The consortium was determined to directly compete against the predominant aircraft of the day. To sustain production, Airbus eyed customers in regions that the major players paid less attention to, such as Asia, Africa, and the Persian Gulf states. It was a sound strategy "that made it possible for Airbus to catch up in a hurry," said William Kovacic, former chairman of the U.S. Federal Trade Commission.

Catch up it did, in good part because of the consortium's successful efforts to reduce aircraft operating and seat-per-mile costs. But Airbus had another important advantage over its American

counterparts: it received hefty subsidies from European governments. This backing would soon take a financial toll on its competitors.

McDonnell Douglas is a case in point, stuck "in a squeeze play between a subsidized European supplier [Airbus] and a much bigger and more successful Boeing," said aviation consultant Loren Thompson. "They simply couldn't generate the resources necessary to match those other two behemoths in all the relevant market sectors."

After years of discounting Airbus as a competitor, Boeing began to pay close attention, particularly when the consortium introduced the Airbus A320 in the late 1980s. More than 400 orders for the jet flew in before its maiden flight in 1987. Among the buyers was United Airlines, until then a major Boeing customer. "It was a shock . . . a strong wake-up call," said former Boeing president and CEO Phil Condit, who succeeded Frank Shrontz in 1996.

The shocks reverberated. Airbus's subsequent A330 family of efficient midsize, wide-body twin jets garnered more than 1,200 airline orders, although the Boeing 777 would overwhelm its sister jet, the four-engine A340. Boeing could no longer dismiss the new antagonist, especially given Airbus's government-funded deep pockets.

As Airbus consumed increasing market share, several U.S. aerospace manufacturers foundered, leading to a progressive series of stunning divestitures, acquisitions, and consolidations. Lockheed Corporation exited the passenger airplane business following the delivery of its last L-1011 TriStar wide-body trijet in 1984, in part because of competition from Airbus. In 1995, Martin Marietta Corporation, which had been created in 1961 with the merger of Glenn L. Martin Company and American-Marietta Corporation, merged with Lockheed to form Lockheed Martin.

The following year, Boeing acquired Rockwell International's aerospace and defense units. At the time, Rockwell was struggling with $2.2 billion in debt, which Boeing agreed to assume in the transaction. The space systems, aircraft division, Rocketdyne, Autonetics, missile systems, and aircraft modification units of Dutch Kindelberger's former company were renamed Boeing North American Inc. and operated as a subsidiary before being fully integrated into the company. The acquisition broadened Boeing's reach into new markets.

These transactions were just a prelude to what would happen next. On December 15, 1996, Boeing announced the biggest aerospace merger in history: a $13.3-billion deal to acquire McDonnell Douglas. The great manufacturer of military and commercial aircraft had struggled to recover from the financial impact of another round of military spending cuts as well as deep incursions by Airbus into its passenger airliner business. Two months earlier, McDonnell Douglas had called off development of the MD-XX superjumbo jet, a derivative of the MD-11 that would have seated 300 to 400 passengers. Earlier that year, the company was unable to advance in the Pentagon's critical Joint Strike Fighter competition, which was held to replace a broad range of existing military fighter aircraft. McDonnell Douglas lost the fly-off stage of the contest to Boeing and Lockheed Martin.

The Boeing–McDonnell Douglas deal was momentous news across the world. Although McDonnell Douglas's commercial airliner business was relatively dormant, the company still enjoyed a premier position as the nation's second-largest defense contractor after Lockheed Martin.

Analysts praised the merger. "The acquisition makes Boeing the only manufacturer of commercial jets in the United States, while catapulting it ahead of the Lockheed Martin Corporation as the world's largest aerospace company," the *New York Times* stated.

Fortune magazine succinctly declared that it was the "sale of the century."

For Boeing, the deal made unquestionable sense: by uniting the companies' product lines and expertise in commercial jetliners *and* military and space aircraft, the combined organization could better ride out these markets' cyclical downturns. In 2000, Boeing further broadened its portfolio with the acquisition of Hughes Space and Communications, maker of the best-selling 601 satellites and the new 702 communications satellites.

Once the dust cleared on the industry's extraordinary consolidation, most of the companies that were the pioneers of the American aircraft manufacturing industry—Boeing, Douglas, McDonnell, and parts of North American Aviation and Hughes Aircraft—had become one. As a new millennium dawned, this powerhouse combination of technological ingenuity, craft, and drive faced the future with tremendous promise—and the knowledge that now, more than ever, the company must compete not just domestically but globally.

The popular McDonnell Douglas (later Boeing) MD-80 jetliner (left) was based on the equally popular Douglas DC-9. More than 1,100 MD-80s were built.

The International Space Station (right) continues to be one of the most complex and internationally cooperative science efforts in history. An artist's conception (left) imagines how scientists might appear through a porthole.

Boeing Today and Tomorrow

After the historic mergers and acquisitions of the 1990s, Boeing's vast workforce stretched across all 50 U.S. states and more than 65 countries. The company had to manage the internal challenges of combining diverse product lines, business processes, and people to succeed in the new era of globalization—with competitors snapping at its heels.

Globalization meant far more than merely selling products to international customers or establishing operations in these countries. The company had to move beyond just conducting commercial transactions toward engaging in a true partnership with its foreign customers and suppliers, becoming more a part of the cultural fabric of the communities with which it did business. Boeing's aim was to make use of the best talent and resources available, no matter where they were located, to advance the company's position at the forefront of innovation.

In this quest, Boeing worked to erase both organizational and geographical boundaries to bring together the ideas of talented people with different backgrounds and experiences across the enterprise. To enhance this global value creation, the company continued to engage in new acquisitions, partnerships, joint ventures, and supplier relationships.

Sending a clear message about the company's new direction, Boeing made the decision in 2001 to relocate company headquarters to Chicago, separate from Boeing's engineering and manufacturing centers in Seattle, St. Louis, and Southern

California. The move signaled to the world that this was a new Boeing.

One of the first projects the new Boeing took on was development of a new commercial airplane—always a risky endeavor. "Commercial aerospace is not a business for the faint of heart," said Harvard Business School professor Willy C. Shih. "The magnitude of investment in new aircraft programs exceeds $20 billion . . . basically 'bet the company' type investments where you may not earn a return for 15 or 20 years. When you get to 15 or 20 years, you'll find out if you had the right product strategy. And if you're wrong—that's a bitter pill to swallow."

Boeing and Airbus reached different conclusions about "the right product strategy." Airbus committed to offering greater passenger capacity, convinced that airlines would continue to fly hub-to-hub routes and serve these hubs through a network of smaller regional routes. To this end, Airbus put the Queen of the Skies herself—Boeing's prized 747 jumbo jet—in its crosshairs by launching the full-length, double-deck A380 superjumbo, which boasted a larger capacity and longer range than the 747.

Boeing took a different tack, emphasizing aircraft speed for swift point-to-point connections in its next-generation airliner, the proposed Sonic Cruiser. The jet was designed with a cruising speed of up to Mach 0.98 (just under the speed of sound) and a passenger capacity of 250. Its unusual design featured a delta wing and small wing-like canards toward the nose, giving it an arrow-like appearance.

The terrorist attacks of September 11, 2001, brought these plans to a sudden halt. Both manufacturers soon confronted the harsh economic realities of the post-9/11 world. Stock markets worldwide suffered unprecedented drops. The price of fuel skyrocketed and the volume of travelers declined, causing several airlines to declare bankruptcy. The airline industry was in chaos.

Previous spread: The 787 Dreamliner has set a new standard for comfort and efficiency in commercial flight.

Right: A rendering of the Sonic Cruiser shows the conceptual aircraft in flight. The plane, which was intended to have a cruising speed of up to Mach .98, was discontinued when Boeing's focus switched to development of the 787.

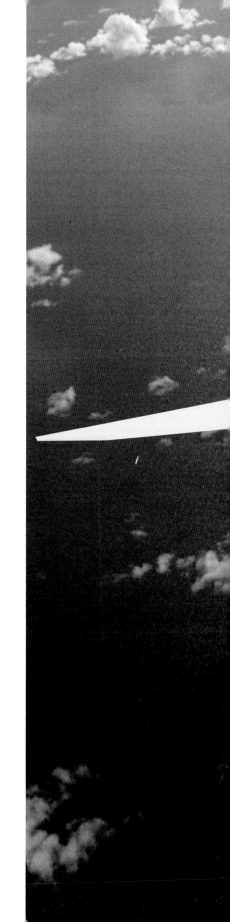

Although the 9/11 attacks did a great deal of damage to the commercial aviation side of the business, Boeing's acquisitions of the previous decade helped mitigate the effect on the overall enterprise. Declines in the airline industry were counterbalanced by sharp increases in military spending, a trend that continued for more than a decade. Contracts for military aircraft and systems such as the Joint Direct Attack Munition (JDAM) weapon system, C-17 Globemaster III transport, F/A-18E/F Super Hornet and F-15E Strike Eagle fighters, and CH-47 Chinook and AH-64 Apache helicopters kept the company on course.

Likewise, the company remained a crucial partner to NASA in programs such as the International Space Station—unquestionably the greatest international cooperative venture in the history of science, technology, and engineering. In addition to designing and building the laboratory module and other major U.S. components of the space station, Boeing was responsible for integration of the hardware and software coming from its many international partners. This meant ensuring that the pieces of the station that were constructed on the ground and transported into space would fit together and function perfectly the first time, a task that made the most of Boeing's proficiency in large-scale systems integration.

While defense forces around the world ramped up and engaged in the global war on terrorism, the airline industry began to regroup. The carriers that remained in operation had little interest in superjumbos like the A380 because of their high operating costs and limited route flexibility. Rather, they sought next-generation aircraft that could do two things much better than current planes could: travel farther on a tank of gas and do so at lower operating costs. Economics became the driver.

Boeing abandoned the Sonic Cruiser design but not its conviction that passengers preferred to fly point-to-point rather than connect through hubs. Opportunely, the company had been simul-taneously developing another type of aircraft using the same technology as the Sonic Cruiser—a conventionally configured yet super-efficient jetliner known initially as the 7E7 (the E stood for "efficiency," among other things).

As work proceeded, the plane was redesignated the 787. It also became the first Boeing commercial airliner in decades to be given a name as well as a number. In 2003, more than half a million people all over the world voted online to choose a name. The winner, Dreamliner, echoed the name of the classic Boeing Stratoliner, the first plane to enter service with a pressurized cabin years before.

The name signaled that, standard appearance aside, the 787 would be a revolutionary airplane using new materials, aircraft systems, and production methods. More important, it would meet airlines' need for a plane that used less fuel while also flying longer routes, reducing environmental impact, and creating a more comfortable flying experience for passengers.

It was an audacious objective, one that would call for the best efforts of Boeing's workforce and an international network of suppliers and partners. And it would be guided by new Boeing chairman and CEO Jim McNerney, who was named to those positions in 2005 after a series of ethics scandals had led to the departure of previous senior executives.

McNerney represented a fresh start for Boeing as the first company leader since Bill Allen to be brought in from outside the organization. At the same time, he was familiar with the industry, having previously led the aircraft engines division of General Electric, and with the company, having served on the Boeing board of directors while he was chairman and CEO of 3M. It was up to the new CEO to establish future strategy, inspire confidence in his mission, and renew the trust of the workforce and Boeing's global partners.

Like other company leaders at critical junctures in Boeing's history, McNerney was both prepared

From wood and cloth to metal to carbon-fiber composites, the physical makeup of airplanes has changed as dramatically as the industry.

for and energized by the challenging duties in front of him. He applied his extensive management experience to operating Boeing more efficiently as a business and unifying the global enterprise into what he called "One Boeing." Such unification was especially needed as Boeing undertook the development of its next commercial airplane—a complex global production effort like no other in the industry's history.

To reduce the weight of the 787, Boeing engineers planned to use composite structural materials to a greater extent than ever before. The 787 represented a reinvention of airplane composition— the second such reinvention in company history. In 1933, Boeing had introduced the first all-metal Model 247, replacing the wood, wire, and muslin planes of the past. Since then, almost all planes had been made of a metal fuselage and metal wings. But that was about to change.

Although the company had successfully used composites in the tail of the 777 and the structures of several military aircraft, Boeing had to assuage potential customer concerns over the use of composite materials in the new jet's fuselage and wings. The overarching question was: would the airlines accept a passenger jetliner made with such a large proportion of unconventional materials?

The company responded creatively to the challenge. While airline executives watched, Boeing representatives took a sledgehammer to a sheet of lightweight composite material. It did not fracture or even chip, alleviating the executives' apprehensions.

Building on their experience with using new materials and computer-aided design and manufacturing on the 777, Boeing engineers designed

the 787 airframe so that nearly half the structure was made from carbon fiber–reinforced plastics and other composites, strong, lightweight materials that allowed for an average 20 percent reduction in aircraft weight compared to more conventional designs.

Manufacturing the composites was as challenging as designing them. Boeing's embrace of globalization allowed an industry-wide collaboration by a multitude of suppliers worldwide, all of them collaborating according to the most stringent timetables. Large composite structures from all over the world were shipped to plants in Charleston, South Carolina, and Everett, Washington, for final assembly.

"Sixty-five percent of the parts were coming in from abroad," said aviation writer Guy Norris. "You're looking at supplies from all around the world . . . that finally have to wind up on that airplane on that day at exactly the right time, in the right sequence. It was a fantastic program and truly representative of the industrial-scale change that Boeing was undertaking."

Many modules, such as the fuselage barrel sections, were extremely large. Ordinarily, these gigantic components would be transported by ship, but this process would take much too long for Boeing to maintain its production schedule. To solve the challenge, the company modified a fleet of four wide-body 747-400 cargo jets, based on a conversion design produced by Boeing's engineering bureau in Moscow, Russia. The company called the cargo freighters Dreamlifters. The Dreamlifters, all of which were operational by 2010, succeeded in their purpose: delivering wings and fuselage barrels built by supply partners in Japan and Italy, respectively, in just hours, as opposed to the more than 30 days it normally took by ship.

An army of international players came together as One Boeing to create the 787. When the first Dreamliner rolled out of production on July 8,

The 787 Dreamliner takes off for the first time as a crowd of Boeing workers and media looks on (left).

Novel features on the 787 include larger windows that can be dimmed electronically (right).

Advanced aerodynamics, propulsion, and electrical power systems increase efficiency and comfort, while reducing noise and emissions.

2007, the milestone was marked with a ceremony attended by roughly 15,000 employees, airline customers, supplier partners, and government dignitaries.

Once complete, the Dreamliner delivered what airlines wanted: a midsize airplane with the range of a big jet, at 20 percent lower fuel consumption and with more cargo revenue capacity than comparably sized aircraft. For passengers, the 787 offered a more comfortable interior that conveyed feelings of spaciousness with higher ceilings, enhanced lighting, increased humidity, and a two-stage cabin air filtration system. Larger windows with novel window dimmers provided near-panoramic views of the horizon.

Newspapers and magazines trumpeted the new jet as a quantum leap forward in aircraft technology. By 2014, the three configurations of the 787 had captured more than 1,000 orders from airlines and leasing companies around the world.

Not everything went smoothly with the delivery of the first Dreamliner. A series of unexpected manufacturing problems led to a three-year delay before the jet finally was delivered to launch customer All Nippon Airways in September 2011. Even after the first planes were delivered, the fleet was grounded for a four-month period due to issues with the innovative lithium-ion batteries.

Once these problems were resolved, the 787 was soon in regular operation with airlines around the world. The new aircraft received high marks from passengers. Boeing quickly ramped up production, turning out more than 10 Dreamliners per month by 2014.

While production of the 787 was picking up, the military side of Boeing saw a downturn be-

cause of cuts in U.S. defense spending. As a result of these cuts, Boeing ceased production of the Collier Award–winning C-17 Globemaster III. However, employment reductions on the defense side were nearly matched by increases in the commercial business.

The company also continued to be active in space exploration and launch systems. In 2006, Boeing and Lockheed Martin became partners in the United Launch Alliance, providing launch services to NASA and the U.S. Department of Defense. The program, which uses Boeing Delta II and Delta IV launch vehicles as well as Atlas V rockets, has sent more than 90 objects into space, including telecommunications satellites and the NASA Mars Exploration Rovers.

As Boeing concludes its first century, it has a balanced, diversified portfolio of products and programs. Using lessons from the development of the 787, the company is refreshing its entire commercial airplane family with offerings such as the 747-8 Intercontinental, 737 MAX, and 777X that provide airlines with greater fuel efficiency and passengers with more comfort. Orders have been robust; in 2013, Boeing booked 1,355 net orders, the second highest number in company history.

Asian markets represent a huge opportunity for Boeing. China is expected to be the world's single largest purchaser of Boeing aircraft in the next two decades, projected to buy as many as 6,000 new jets at a combined value of approximately $780 billion. The company has sold aircraft to China since President Richard Nixon's historic 1972 visit to the country resulted in a deal for China to buy 10 707s. Boeing has maintained strong relations with the country, assisting in the building of its aerospace infrastructure, helping train its pilots, and guiding its regulatory equivalent of the FAA. Although China has ambitions to become a competitor at some point, Boeing's preeminent technologies and unparalleled skill sets have given the company a long lead.

The 787 Dreamliner, with components made all over the world, exemplifies the globalization of the aviation industry. The Dreamlifter (right) is a specially modified 747 cargo jet that is large enough to carry 787 wings and fuselages from overseas to the United States for final assembly.

On the defense side, Boeing continues to be the nation's number-two contractor, managing a diverse portfolio of programs with U.S. and international governments for leading-edge fighters, helicopters, and launch systems—as well as newer endeavors such as cybersecurity and global support and logistics that are a natural extension of the company's expertise in computing and large-scale systems integration. Looking to the future, Boeing and Lockheed Martin are following up their successful partnership on the U.S. Air Force F-22 Raptor tactical fighter by teaming up for the Air Force's Long-Range Strike Bomber competition.

In addition to conventional fighters and other aircraft, Boeing is now providing an important new tool in the U.S. Navy's defense arsenal: the P-8 Poseidon, nicknamed the "sub hunter," a military derivative of the 737-800 (with 737-900 wings) designed to conduct anti-submarine warfare, anti-surface warfare, shipping interdiction, and electronic signals intelligence. Another commercial-defense crossover is the Boeing KC-46 Pegasus aerial tanker for the U.S. Air Force, derived from the venerable 767 jetliner.

Boeing continues to pursue innovative technologies that will enable humankind to fly higher, farther, and faster. Boeing's Phantom Works division, whose name echoes that of the famous F-4 Phantom II combat jet, is the advanced prototyping arm of the company's defense and security enterprises. The division gathers wide-ranging skill sets from throughout the global enterprise for a single purpose: to break through technological barriers to develop singular technologies into

prototypes. If all goes according to plan, these prototypes are then transformed into actual products.

One such prototype from Phantom Works is the Boeing Phantom Eye, a high-altitude, long-endurance unmanned aerial vehicle (UAV) designed to provide advanced intelligence and reconnaissance. Phantom Eye uses a liquid hydrogen propulsion system to achieve flights of up to four days at high altitude. Another revolutionary concept is the X-51 WaveRider, an experimental UAV whose name derives from its inventive use of sonic shock waves to add lift to the aircraft. A supersonic combustion ramjet engine called a scramjet powers the UAV, using hydrocarbon fuel to reach hypersonic speeds (Mach 5 and higher). Unlike conventional rocket engines, the scramjet engine does not require oxygen tanks, instead harvesting oxygen as it flies through the atmosphere.

In 2013, the X-51 reached Mach 5.1, approximately 4,000 miles per hour, flying over the Pacific Ocean. With experimental tests now successfully concluded, its legacy is the depth of knowledge it is providing to scientists designing and developing hypersonic aircraft for the future.

"We're extremely excited about it," said former U.S. Air Force Lieutenant General David Deptula. "If you can fly at hypersonic speeds for minutes and then can do [the same thing for] hours, it [creates] the ability to get anywhere on the surface of the Earth rapidly, which opens up an entirely new spectrum of capabilities."

An equally important initiative at Boeing is the creation of cleaner, more efficient products. Boeing is leading a global aerospace industry effort to develop more sustainable aviation biofuels that reduce carbon emissions and the industry's reliance on fossil fuels. Under a contract with NASA, Boeing also is conducting research for the Subsonic Ultra Green Aircraft Research (SUGAR) program, developing the SUGAR Volt concept vehicle, a twin-engine aircraft that uses hybrid

The KC-46A Pegasus (left) extends Boeing's 50-year franchise in aerial refueling tankers, which began with a modified B-29 Superfortress.

The Boeing 502 small satellite, seen at right in an artist's rendering, will carry the first high-resolution hyperspectral payload.

electric engines and an innovative truss-based wing to decrease fuel consumption.

Working in partnership with American Airlines and with funding from the Federal Aviation Administration, Boeing also converted a 737 jetliner into an ecoDemonstrator to test a variety of advanced technologies designed to reduce the environmental impact of commercial aircraft.

Years after the last shuttle flight, Boeing continues to be involved in manned and unmanned space exploration programs. The International Space Station supports a wide range of scientific experiments in micro-gravity conditions and is expected to be a gateway to deeper space destinations, including the moon and eventually Mars. The company's contributions to research integration support and payload development services will enable the station to remain fully operational through 2024.

Boeing also has contracts to support work on the NASA Orion Multi-Purpose Crew Vehicle (MPCV)—the next-generation manned spacecraft—as well as the new NASA Space Launch System (SLS) that will take Orion and its crew to the International Space Station, the moon, and even Mars.

In 2014, Boeing was selected by NASA to manufacture the CST-100 vehicle to transport passengers and cargo to the International Space Station and other planned commercial space stations in support of NASA's Commercial Crew Program. Boeing space exploration engineers partnered with its commercial airplane designers to adapt the passenger-pleasing cabin layout

The Boeing Phantom Works X-51 WaveRider, an experimental unmanned aerial vehicle that uses its own hypersonic shockwaves for lift and travels at more than five times the speed of sound, is shown in an artist's rendering.

and lighting of today's Boeing airliners to the new space vehicle.

The company's satellite business has progressed at a rapid pace in recent years. Since the beginning of the Global Positioning System (GPS) program in 1974, Boeing has built 40 of the 62 satellites launched in the series operated by the U.S. Air Force. In 2008, Boeing constructed a 20,500-square-foot satellite mission control center in El Segundo, California, to manage up to four commercial or government satellite missions at one time. Two years later, the company developed and built the first GPS IIF satellite, launched in May 2010 to enhance navigation and positioning accuracy on Earth. Boeing is under contract to build another 11 of the satellites.

Despite the U.S. aerospace industry's consolidation following a historic spate of mergers and acquisitions, global competition is expected to increase. Although Boeing's chief rival today in the commercial airliner space is Airbus, new competitors are emerging in Brazil, Russia, Japan, and China. On the military side, Lockheed Martin and Northrop Grumman are Boeing's top competitors, although there are other international players. With entrepreneurs including Richard Branson and Elon Musk now taking an interest in commercial space travel, Boeing has a potential new market—and new challengers.

In 2012, Boeing regained its market share leadership in commercial airplanes, which it had lost to Airbus in 2004. Today, Boeing is the world's largest, most diverse aerospace company. A true global enterprise, Boeing continues to build

The largest and most powerful rocket ever built, the Space Launch System (SLS) will enable NASA to make manned missions to Mars. Boeing is the primary contractor for the SLS core stage.

strong business momentum across the world. "It used to be winning in America meant you won everywhere," said Boeing chairman and CEO Jim McNerney. "Today, you have to win everywhere to win in America."

A century is a long time for any business to survive. For a company to thrive that long in the aerospace industry is an extraordinary achievement. From its humble beginnings in a boathouse, The Boeing Company has endured to become the world's premier aerospace company, the largest manufacturer of commercial jetliners and military aircraft combined, and the United States' biggest exporter. A company that once made biplanes of wood and fabric now manufactures jets of composite materials that didn't exist a century ago. From a single customer in the U.S. government, Boeing now tallies thousands of customers in 145 countries.

Along the way, Boeing has pushed through boundaries that were thought to be impenetrable. The company led the manufacture of military aircraft in World War II and made good on a young American president's plan to put humans on the moon. At great financial risk, it manufactured the first swept-wing jet and the wide-body Queen of the Skies. Even when it fell flat—when competitors beat it to the gate with a better model, when gov-

Phantom Eye (left) is an unmanned reconnaissance vehicle powered by liquid hydrogen under development at Boeing Phantom Works. The larger scale version will eventually be capable of up to ten days of autonomous flight without refueling.

ernment regulations forced its hasty breakup, or when foreign policy and global economics conspired against its business—the people of Boeing persevered, learned from these setbacks, and did what they had set out to do: make better aircraft.

In the 100 years since Boeing opened for business, it has welcomed hundreds of thousands of workers. Indeed, the company's long history has been shaped as much by these individuals' ingenuity, dedication, and integrity as by their innovative solutions to vexing problems. Time and again, the company's skilled leadership, ability to reposition quickly, employees' can-do resolve, and passion to satisfy customer needs have lifted Boeing.

Since the dawn of the 20th century, Boeing has explored and embraced new technologies that improve the way we live, communicate, and travel. In the 21st century, last century's aviation giants—Boeing, Douglas, McDonnell, North American, and Hughes, now united as a global enterprise—continue on this journey.

Bill Boeing first articulated the company's basic philosophy a century ago: "We are embarked as pioneers upon a new science and industry in which our problems are so new and unusual that it behooves no one to dismiss any novel idea with the statement 'It can't be done.'" It is this philosophy that continues to drive Boeing today.

When complete, the 777X series (shown here in an artist's rendering) will be the world's largest and most-efficient twin-engine jet.

Index

City lights shine in a satellite view of Earth. Aerospace innovations have connected people all over the globe, from the airplanes that traverse the planet in a matter of hours to satellites that transmit data from place to place in mere seconds.

Photo Credits

Acknowledgments

All images courtesy of and copyright ©
The Boeing Company unless noted below:

Pages 14–15: Courtesy of NASA
Page 62: Courtesy of the Library of Congress
Page 81: The George Schairer Collection/The
Museum of Flight
Page 118: Courtesy of NASA
Page 126: Courtesy of NASA
Page 127: Courtesy of NASA
Page 128: Courtesy of NASA
Page 129: Courtesy of NASA
Page 131: Courtesy of NASA
Page 169: Courtesy of NASA
Page 184: Courtesy of the U.S. Air Force
Pages 190–191: Courtesy of NASA

Jacket back, center image: Courtesy of NASA

The writing of this book would not have been possible without the support of a team of contributors and reviewers, including Daniel Beck, Charles Bickers, John Dern, Tom Downey, Carrie Kipp Howard, Jim Newcomb, Paul Proctor, Erik Simonsen, and Anne Toulouse at Boeing; Boeing historians and archivists Michael J. Lombardi, Henry Brownlee Jr., and Patricia McGinnis; editor Kristin Mehus-Roe; designer Zach Hooker; photo researcher Jessica Eskelsen; Pamela Geismar and Beth Weber with Chronicle Books; and the many photographers and artists whose work is displayed in these pages.